"*The Heart of Business* will be the defining business book of this decade. Hubert Joly shares his highly successful, simple, profound insights that reprioritize purpose, people, and profit. His proven philosophies are a brilliant guide for all leaders and companies preparing to rapidly pivot toward serving all stakeholders in this new age of inclusive capitalism."

—ANGELA AHRENDTS, former Senior Vice President,
    Apple Retail; former CEO, Burberry

"*The Heart of Business* makes it clear that Hubert Joly knows what it takes to create an environment in which every unique individual is valued for who they are and what they bring to the table. He knows that diversity is not an afterthought but a fundamental business imperative. He knows how to lead with purpose and humanity. And by reading *The Heart of Business*, so will you."

—CRYSTAL E. ASHBY, Interim President and CEO,
    The Executive Leadership Council (ELC)

"This book, written by one of the most compelling and compassionate CEOs in a generation, will serve as a guide for all who aspire to lead with purpose and live a professional life filled with meaning. I witnessed this firsthand as Hubert led a once-in-a-lifetime retail turnaround that was grounded, first and foremost, on the principle that purpose is as important as profit and that the work itself, while hard, can be joyful and filled with heart."

—CORIE BARRY, CEO, Best Buy

"Putting purpose and people first is the most powerful driver of performance and long-term value: this is Hubert Joly's core message. His approach, his vision of companies as a community of their stakeholders, and his call for agility and empowerment resonate deeply with my own experience heading a company that has people at its heart. This is a must-read and an inspiration for any leader wanting to make a positive economic, social, and environmental impact."

—SOPHIE BELLON, Chairwoman, Sodexo

"Best Buy's turnaround under Hubert Joly's leadership was remarkable—a case study that should and will be taught in business schools around the world. Bold and thoughtful—he has a lot to teach."

—JEFF BEZOS, founder and CEO, Amazon

"The quest for meaning, and with it, questions about leadership and purpose in business, may very well be capitalism's most pressing issue today. Drawing on his inspiring journey as Chair and CEO of Best Buy, Hubert Joly describes how placing people and their aspirations at the core of companies is the key to aligning personal fulfilment, business success, and a positive impact on the world. *The Heart of Business* does much more than provide useful management principles and advice, though: it also nudges us to think about the meaning of life itself. With experience and wisdom, Hubert Joly makes a crucial contribution to the future of capitalism."

—THOMAS BUBERL, CEO, AXA

"Hubert Joly's *The Heart of Business* is both timely and timeless. A perfect leadership book for our era, it will help leaders across the world and at every level tap into the enduring truths about how to inspire people. Hubert's own transformation from a highly analytical, hard-charging McKinsey consultant into a purpose-led leader, brought to life in the book with memorable stories and true humility, shows readers why pursuing a noble purpose and putting people at the center is an extraordinary leadership formula open to everyone."

—JAMES M. CITRIN, Leader, CEO Practice, Spencer Stuart; author,
    You're in Charge—Now What?

"This book is a must-have for current or aspiring leaders. Having seen Hubert 'in action' as a fellow CEO, I am even more inspired reading about the principles that have guided him. *The Heart of Business* underscores the critical importance of human-centric management to foster growth and to ensure business is a genuine force of good— something our world desperately needs."

—MARY DILLON, CEO, Ulta Beauty

"Hubert Joly is a leader I deeply respect and admire. This compelling book captures his gift of using purpose and inspiring human connections with employees, customers, suppliers, investors, and communities. A must-read if you want to learn how to do this effectively."

—JOHN DONAHOE, President and CEO, Nike

"Hubert Joly's outstanding *The Heart of Business* will do for you what meeting and learning from him have done for me: it will truly and fully transform your approach to work, leadership, and life."

—RODOLPHE DURAND, professor and Joly Family Purposeful Leadership Chair, HEC Paris

"Leaders often focus on the technology and business transformations underway. In *The Heart of Business*, Hubert Joly shows us what true and effective leadership is really about: articulating a noble purpose, putting people at the center, embracing all stakeholders, and treating profit as an outcome."

—AICHA EVANS, CEO, Zoox

"After reviving multiple companies, Hubert Joly now takes on his biggest challenge: turning around capitalism itself. *The Heart of Business* is more than a management treatise or memoir. It is an exploration of how business can help people find meaning and purpose—and how companies themselves can identify their own noble purpose to guide them forward. Joly makes a compelling, business-oriented case for why the future of capitalism depends on helping people flourish at work."

—ROGER W. FERGUSON JR., President and CEO, TIAA

"Hubert Joly is one of the most gifted leaders of our time, with an extraordinary ability to navigate unimaginable business challenges while simultaneously lifting others around him to fulfill a higher purpose. *The Heart of Business* provides a practical and aspirational road map for all leaders to elevate their impact by focusing first on what matters most—the power of human connection. There is no better teacher than Hubert to inspire all of us to lead with vulnerability, empathy, and courage."

—MICHELLE GASS, CEO, Kohl's

"The amazing saga of Best Buy, led by Hubert Joly and his team, is one of the most inspiring and instructional stories of this century. *The Heart of Business* is a must-read book for leaders at all levels, in any organization! It is a road map for anyone who wants to become a leader of the future."

—MARSHALL GOLDSMITH, number one *New York Times*–bestselling author, *Triggers* and *What Got You Here Won't Get You There*

"Hubert Joly is a refreshing voice on organizational transformation, and with *The Heart of Business* he now shares an equally visionary perspective on the next potential phase of stakeholder capitalism. This is must-read material for anyone looking to understand modern business as a force for global good, the changing nature of leadership, and why deep purpose needs to be at the heart of everything we do."

—ALEX GORSKY, Chairman and CEO, Johnson & Johnson

"In his inspiring and transformative book, *The Heart of Business*, Hubert Joly uses his years of experience at Best Buy to clearly show the importance of purposeful and human leadership and how to implement it. This playbook for 'unleashing human magic' will change hearts and minds not only on how companies are run but how business and capitalism are taught in business schools. This is a must-read and a defining book of our time."

—ARIANNA HUFFINGTON, founder and CEO, Thrive Global

"*The Heart of Business* is a clarion call to rethink why and how we do business. Hubert Joly's leadership and humanity shine on every page, and his philosophy, shared through stories of the experiences and people who shaped it, has produced spectacular success. This book is as inspiring, authentic, and approachable as the author himself."

—CINDY KENT, Executive Vice President and President,
Senior Living, Brookdale

"Hubert Joly turns traditional business concepts on their heads to prove that leading with purpose and heart to serve all stakeholders, not just shareholders, builds the most long-term value for any organization. *The Heart of Business* reveals why transformation starts with people and how it results in financial success. This practical and actionable guide is a must-read for any leader striving for inspiration and extraordinary results."

—LINDA KOZLOWSKI, President and CEO, Blue Apron

"In business, certain principles are musts for any CEO to be successful. Hubert Joly, fresh from his incredible success in Best Buy's turnaround, clearly enunciates these principles: pursue a noble purpose, make your employees feel important in the mission, include all stakeholders, and—if carried out correctly—the outcome will be substantial profits. This book is a road map for success in running any business, large or small."

—HENRY KRAVIS, cofounder, KKR

"The philosophy of Hubert Joly's *The Heart of Business* is from his heart and one he has shared personally as a director of our company for over a decade. His belief that the journey to success is led by pursuing a noble purpose and putting people first is part of what he calls 'human magic.' The resurgence of Best Buy under his former leadership is just one example of the transformative power of those heartfelt principles. Over these many years it has been my privilege to be inspired by Hubert's honest sharing of these experiences firsthand. *The Heart of Business* is a unique and very human guide to true leadership and ways to work together, especially during these challenging times."

—RALPH LAUREN, Executive Chairman and Chief Creative Officer, Ralph Lauren Corporation

"Fairy tale in business? No! A great, true story of effectiveness and great results. *The Heart of Business* is a must-read: Hubert Joly shares how he changed Best Buy by doing good and making employees happier and more passionate about their brand, the products, the customers, and the stores."

—MAURICE LÉVY, Chairman of the Supervisory Board, Publicis Groupe

"The *Heart of Business* is a modern business guide that demonstrates the power of purpose and people to unlock value for all stakeholders. It delivers invaluable firsthand insight from Hubert Joly's transformative journey at Best Buy and elsewhere and reminds us that strategy is nothing more than words on paper until it is activated by 'human magic.' Hubert's thoughtful message is an inspiring and highly compelling call to action for any leader."

—PATRICE LOUVET, President and CEO, Ralph Lauren

"For more than a decade, I have watched with great admiration as Hubert Joly put his unique vision of how to lead into practice. In this book, he captures the core principles and experiences that made him so successful as a leader. By combining reflections with pragmatic examples that focus on the importance of purpose and people, Hubert has created the ultimate guide for the twenty-first-century leader."

—BILL MCNABB, former Chairman and CEO, Vanguard

"In *The Heart of Business,* Hubert Joly distills a lifetime of lessons about business, leadership, and life. This is a relevant, compelling, and timely book from a courageous leader!"

—ALAN MULALLY, former CEO, Ford Motor Company and Boeing Commercial Airplanes

"Bravo, Hubert Joly! At last, here is a CEO who demonstrates how a business with employees aligned behind an inspiring purpose can enjoy unexpected, transformational success. Hubert Joly breaks the mold by boldly asserting—and proving—that heart, humanity, and even magic are essential to stakeholders' engagement and to sustained performance. If broadly practiced, this fresh and enlightened approach will make business a force for good and may even save capitalism."

—MARILYN CARLSON NELSON, former Chair and CEO, Carlson

"Through great storytelling and lessons from his own experience, Hubert invites us to think deeply about a company's purpose—to contribute to the common good and serve all its stakeholders in a harmonious fashion by unleashing human magic—and offers a set of principles and practical advice on how to make this vision a reality."

—SATYA NADELLA, CEO, Microsoft

"I've had the good fortune of knowing Hubert for over a decade. *The Heart of Business* is a thought-provoking read on the notion that noble purpose is an essential driver of business success today. He reinforces this thesis with compelling anecdotes from his illustrious career and provides a practical guide to putting it into action. It is a timely and meaningful book that reminds us of the vital role companies can play in moving the world forward."

—SHANTANU NARAYEN, CEO, Adobe Systems

"In *The Heart of Business,* Hubert Joly shares his principles about business and leadership, how he came to shape them, and how he has been putting them to work over the years. Whether you are fresh out of business school or a seasoned CEO, this is a wonderful book to include in your reading list."

—INDRA NOOYI, former Chairman and CEO, PepsiCo

"As leaders and organizations look to create and nurture meaning for themselves, their employees, their customers, and the world, the lessons from Hubert Joly's *The Heart of Business* are more powerful than ever. Drawing on stories from a life well lived—and organizations well led—Joly's treatise inspires both new and seasoned leaders to consider why we work and how we can do so with power, heart, and purpose. Joly reminds us that reconnecting with what matters is what truly makes work *work*."

—ERIC PLINER, CEO, YSC Consulting

"Hubert Joly is a revered leader who has unequivocally proven the business case for stakeholder capitalism. This book captures his passion for purpose and people above profits and, just when humanity is at its most vulnerable, showcases with unique insight and practical examples how to make business an unstoppable force for good."

—PAUL POLMAN, cofounder and Chair, IMAGINE; former CEO, Unilever

"Hubert Joly proves that businesses don't need to choose between profit and purpose. But more than that, he shows us how it's done, with practical advice and clear examples. It's hard not to feel optimistic about the future of capitalism after reading this book."

—GINNI ROMETTY, former CEO, IBM; Cochair, OneTen

"People first! This book will bring back hope to those who doubt the sustainability of capitalism. Brilliantly illustrated by numerous heartfelt examples from his own professional life, Hubert Joly explains how a purposeful human organization, based on caring and trust, can turn the most desperate company into an industry leader. No surprise that Hubert Joly is one of the most respected business leaders today. He convincingly lays the path forward for business, and his advice should be followed."

—JEAN-DOMINIQUE SENARD, Chairman, Renault

"Business should be a force for good. Hubert Joly has shown that putting purpose and people at *The Heart of Business* is the best kind of executive leadership."

—KEVIN SNEADER, Global Managing Partner, McKinsey & Company

"*The Heart of Business* unveils a new paradigm of leadership for the twenty-first century, at odds with traditional thinking. It emphasizes purpose and its necessary alignment with people and culture. A new leadership approach is needed, focusing on long-term and sustainable performance and giving strong meaning to the contribution of everyone. Hubert's book describes a positive path for business, based on the diverse experience of his rich career and a profound conviction of the difference people make in our companies."

—JEAN-PASCAL TRICOIRE, Chairman and CEO, Schneider Electric

"Long before stakeholder capitalism and the idea of purpose in business were being talked about, Hubert Joly was already embracing both with impressive success. One of the very best business leaders now lifts the veil on why leading with purpose and humanity makes sense, along with how to make it work in the real world. Thoughtful, well researched, very practical, and eminently readable, *The Heart of Business* offers a joyful and inspiring vision of how to reinvent business and capitalism from the heart."

—DARREN WALKER, President, Ford Foundation

HUBERT JOLY

WITH CAROLINE LAMBERT

THE
HEART OF
BUSINESS

LEADERSHIP PRINCIPLES FOR
THE NEXT ERA OF CAPITALISM

HARVARD BUSINESS REVIEW PRESS

Boston, Massachusetts

Copyright 2021 Hubert Joly
All rights reserved
Printed in the United States of America

10 9 8

No part of this publication may be reproduced, stored in or introduced into a retrieval system, or transmitted, in any form or by any means (electronic, mechanical, photocopying, recording, or otherwise) without the prior permission of the publisher. Requests for permission should be directed to permissions@harvardbusiness.org or mailed to Permissions, Harvard Business School Publishing, 60 Harvard Way, Boston, Massachusetts 02163.

The web addresses referenced in this book were live and correct at the time of the book's publication but may be subject to change.

Library of Congress Cataloging-in-Publication Data

Names: Joly, Hubert, author. | Lambert, Caroline.
Title: The heart of business : leadership principles for the next era of capitalism / Hubert Joly with Caroline Lambert.
Description: Boston, MA : Harvard Business Review Press, [2021] | Includes index.
Identifiers: LCCN 2020047842 (print) | LCCN 2020047843 (ebook) | ISBN 9781647820381 (hardcover) | ISBN 9781647820398 (ebook)
Subjects: LCSH: Best Buy (Firm) | Business ethics. | Industrial management. | Psychology, Industrial. | Leadership. | Success in business.
Classification: LCC HF5387 .J647 2021 (print) | LCC HF5387 (ebook) | DDC 658.4/092—dc23
LC record available at https://lccn.loc.gov/2020047842
LC ebook record available at https://lccn.loc.gov/2020047843

ISBN: 978-1-64782-038-1

eISBN: 978-1-64782-039-8

The paper used in this publication meets the requirements of the American National Standard for Permanence of Paper for Publications and Documents in Libraries and Archives Z39.48-1992.

To Hortense

CONTENTS

FOREWORD

by Bill George

I am honored to have the opportunity to write this foreword for my good friend Hubert Joly's masterpiece, *The Heart of Business*. This book should become the guiding light for a new generation of business leaders who will revitalize capitalism around their employees, customers, suppliers, and communities while realizing sustainable returns for their investors.

This is not your typical book by a former CEO. Instead, Hubert weaves his lifetime of experience in the trenches of global business with deep personal wisdom. In doing so, he models a way of leading that all business leaders should pursue.

Arriving at the point where he could write such an important book was not an easy path. Hubert is a learner who courageously took on challenging turnaround roles in industries where he had no prior experience. He used his rigorous French education and elite training as a McKinsey consultant to lead five companies as CEO, culminating in the transformation of Best Buy. During these years, Hubert went through a personal transformation, from seeking to be the smartest person at the table to becoming a passionate and compassionate leader of people.

Hubert and I met shortly after he moved to Minneapolis as CEO of Carlson Companies, and we became neighbors. We learned we had much in common in our beliefs about leadership, the purpose of capitalism, and what is required to build and sustain great companies. We had followed similar paths through the corporate world—Hubert in France and I in America—learning the hard way that leadership is not about being the person who has all the answers.

By the time Hubert became CEO of Best Buy in 2012, he had led turnarounds as head of EDS France, Vivendi's video game division, Carlson Wagonlit Travel, and Carlson Companies. Despite his achievements at EDS and Vivendi, by his early forties he was feeling disillusioned from chasing success. This is what inspired him to take "a step back and spend time looking into my soul to find a better direction for my life." In his study with Catholic monks and a number of CEOs in France, he realized that work is a noble calling to serve others and an expression of love. Quoting the poet Khalil Gibran, who wrote, "Work is love made visible," Hubert believes work must be guided by the pursuit of a purpose with people at its center. This conviction has shaped his life and his career.

In *The Heart of Business*, Hubert shares all aspects of his personal journey to his heart, as he learned that engaging people in a shared mission was a more powerful way to lead. As a private person, he found out that sharing his vulnerabilities connected him to people in a deeper way and encouraged them to be open with him. He writes, "There can be no genuine human connection without vulnerability, and no vulnerability without imperfections."

Hubert was not alone in having mid-career feelings of reaching the mountaintop at a young age and asking, "Is this all there is?" I too felt this way in my forties in my later years at Honeywell. Immersed in my third consecutive turnaround, I was striving to become CEO of this global company. One day while driving home in 1988, I looked in the rearview mirror and saw a miserable person. I finally admitted to myself that I was losing my way, striving to win a title in a business I wasn't passionate about, rather than fulfilling my calling. Instead of leading with my heart, I was suppressing my passion and compassion. Thanks to my wife's urging and encouragement from my men's group, that wake-up call led me to accept Medtronic's offer, where I spent the best 13 years of my professional career.

In 1995, my wife, Penny, and I met with Buddhist monk Thich Nhat Hanh, who taught us, "The longest journey you will ever take is the 18 inches from your head to your heart." Yet wisdom gained on the journey does not always translate immediately into action. Even as CEO of Medtronic, I was still learning that lesson. Although I had worked on making that journey to my heart, I realized I had a way to go. In a similar fashion, Hubert provides a refreshing perspective for someone who has been so successful. The key lesson is to have an open heart and a beginner's mind as you journey inward to discover your authentic self.

Just as Hubert's personal journey transformed his leadership to be more heart centered, so did his philosophy of leadership. Through his experiences, he recognized companies must undertake their own journeys as well—moving from pursuing financial goals to discovering that the heart of business resides in its people. Hubert observes that "corporations are not soulless entities, but human organizations with people at their center, working together in support of that purpose." When companies do this, it unleashes "human magic" by creating an environment where all employees can blossom and reach their full potential. He argues that central to every business is its purpose, which enables the organization to contribute to the common good and serve all its stakeholders.

Given the dire straits Best Buy was in, many analysts were predicting in 2012 it would go out of business or be taken apart by a private equity firm. After Hubert was elected CEO, he and I spent many hours together discussing the challenges he faced. Most CEOs asked to lead such a turnaround would follow the conventional corporate turnaround playbook: (1) close 30–40% of stores and sell real estate, (2) terminate 30,000–40,000 employees, (3) narrow product categories, (4) squeeze suppliers for lower prices, and (5) then get paid a large incentive.

Hubert took a different tack—recognizing that purpose and people were the key to unleashing the energy required to undertake the difficult task of turning the business around. Acknowledging he knew little about the retail business, he became a learner, traveling to St. Cloud, Minnesota, dressed in khaki pants and the iconic Best Buy Blue Shirt with a tag that read "CEO in Training." There he spent his first four days at Best Buy understanding what was wrong through the eyes of customers and frontline employees.

Hubert inspired Best Buy's employees to engage in Best Buy's turnaround strategy, "Renew Blue." His priorities were building Best Buy's revenues and improving its margins, with reducing jobs and closing stores as the last resort. He did so by creating a positive environment and being fully transparent about the company's challenges.

Turnarounds can take a long time—a time filled with uncertainty—so Hubert looked for small wins to celebrate publicly, such as announcing flat sales at the end of 2012, signaling that revenue declines were over. Instead of squeezing suppliers, he partnered with them—even arch-rival Amazon—by using floor space to create "mini-stores" for Samsung, Microsoft, and Apple, and adding appliances and health care. These steps gave Best Buy's 125,000 employees reason for hope and rewards for their hard work, creating the "human magic" he was after.

As a result, increased sales and margin improvements strengthened the company's depressed stock price, rewarding its shareholders. With Best Buy's turnaround complete by 2016, Hubert guided the crafting of the company's mission "to enrich customers' lives through technology" as he shifted to its growth strategy, "Building the New Blue."

While much can be learned from Hubert's successful turnaround of Best Buy, *The Heart of Business* has so much more to offer. Its most meaningful messages address what it will take for organizations to succeed in the years ahead by inspiring employees to align in pursuit of a common purpose. By enabling employees to realize their work fulfills a noble purpose, he calls for a refocusing of companies around employees in service to customers and the common good.

Hubert makes a compelling case that pursuing a company's purpose is superior to Milton Friedman's dictate that "the social responsibility of business is to increase its profits." He believes, and I agree, that sustainable profits are the successful outcome of organizations that are mission driven and focus on all their stakeholders.

In the future, every company will need to focus on its purpose, or raison d'être, in order to establish legitimacy in serving society by creating value for all stakeholders. Companies that follow Hubert's approach will provide rewarding work and well-paying jobs for their employees, products and services that enhance and improve their customers' lives, and sustainable returns for their investors, thus becoming the force for good needed to transform society.

Hubert Joly has shown us the way to achieve this vision in a magnificent book that encapsulates all his philosophies into an integrated whole. If business leaders heed its messages and pursue this approach, the world will be a lot better for it.

Bill George is senior fellow at Harvard Business School, former Chair and CEO of Medtronic, and author of Discover Your True North.

Introduction

"Jim, you're crazy!"

This is what I said to my friend Jim Citrin, who leads the North American CEO practice at Spencer Stuart, the global executive search company. Jim and I had known each other since the 1980s, when we both worked at management consulting firm McKinsey & Company. It was May 2012, and Jim had asked me a simple question: Would I be interested in becoming the next CEO of Best Buy?

I had known Best Buy for a long time, and not just because I was living in Minnesota when I got Jim's call. A dozen years earlier, when I was leading the video games division of Vivendi Universal out of Los Angeles, I had first braved the winters in Minneapolis to pitch *Diablo II*, *Half-Life*, or some other of our latest video games at Best Buy's headquarters. Undeterred by the climate, I moved to Minneapolis in 2008 to become the CEO of Carlson Companies. A year later, I asked Brad Anderson, who had just stepped down as Best Buy CEO after 35 years in the company, to join the board of Carlson because I greatly admired how he and Best Buy founder Dick Schulze had built a formidable retail powerhouse. Starting as one single outlet selling audio equipment in St. Paul, Minnesota, Best Buy had become the largest chain of consumer electronics stores in the world.

But Jim's idea did feel insane, no matter how I looked at it. I knew nothing about retail, and by 2012, Best Buy's market dynamics were not looking good: online retailers, particularly Amazon, were fast disrupting electronics retail, leaving once powerful brands struggling. Circuit City had already filed for bankruptcy, and Radio Shack was heading in the same direction. In addition, several of Best Buy's most important vendors—Apple, Microsoft, Sony, and others—were establishing their own stores. At the same time, Best Buy's operational performance had been deteriorating in the domestic market for several years as the company looked to expand internationally.

If all that weren't enough, the CEO had just been fired; founder Dick Schulze wanted to take the company private; and analysts and investors were predicting that Best Buy was on its way to extinction.

"It's a complete zoo!" I told Jim.

He was having none of it, though. "It is a perfect fit for you. This is a turnaround situation, and you are a brilliant turnaround guy. I think it could be great! You should at least take a look."

Three things led me to decide to follow Jim's advice and investigate. One, I was open to leave Carlson after eight years, as the Carlson family and I had different views of how the business should move forward. Two, I trusted Jim. Three, I had indeed led several turnarounds in my life, and I could see how my experience in a number of disrupted industries and sectors analogous or adjacent to Best Buy's could be relevant and helpful.

I conducted the type of due diligence one typically does in this situation. I read everything I could about Best Buy. I listened to investor presentations. I spoke with people who had worked there. I visited some stores. And the more I learned, the more excited I became.

Amazon was not the problem. Neither was the market or digital disruption.

In fact, it was an exciting time in the market, as innovation in consumer technology was driving significant demand. I thought that the world needed Best Buy: customers needed help with their technology choices, and vendors needed this extensive network of stores to showcase the fruit of their billions of dollars of R&D investment. I still did not know much about the retail business, but it was clear to me that, although Best Buy faced significant challenges, its problems were in large part self-inflicted—and therefore entirely within the company's control. Best Buy's future did not have to be an inevitable demise. This could be fixed!

By the time I first met the Best Buy board members who would select the next CEO, I no longer thought Jim was crazy. I wanted the job.

"I feel I have spent my entire professional life preparing for this job," I told board member Kathy Higgins Victor and the rest of the search committee during my first interview with them on July 14, 2012 (Bastille Day—always significant for a Frenchman). The following month—on my birthday—I received a call from Kathy, who told me I would be the next CEO of Best Buy.

The next eight years at Best Buy were an inspiring and fulfilling adventure. The company that Amazon was supposed to kill became once again a thriving, growing retailer, partnering with Amazon itself and staffed with dedicated, fired-up employees. By June 2019, when I passed the CEO baton to Corie Barry and her leadership team, Best Buy had recorded six straight years of growth; earnings had tripled; and the share price, which slouched toward single digits in 2012, reached $75. Media reports spoke of how we "defied expectations," "broke the mold," and "rescued the company." I felt I had accomplished what I had set out to do. Then in June 2020, I stepped down as chairman.

During my time at the company, I was able to put into practice what I had learned earlier in my career, and I also learned an enormous amount from the people of Best Buy. I learned about work, about the nature and role of companies, and about what lights the kind of fire within employees that results in exceptional performance. I also learned about leadership.

I learned that so much of what I had been taught about business at business school and as a consultant and young executive is either wrong, outdated, or incomplete. I learned that the purpose of a company is not to make money, contrary to what Milton Friedman wanted us to believe. I learned that the old top-down approach to management—having a few smart executives first formulate a strategy and its implementation plan, then tell everybody else in the company what to do while crafting incentives to motivate them—rarely works. And I learned that the model of the leader as a smart, powerful superhero is outdated.

Through all my experiences, culminating in the incredible years at Best Buy, I have come to believe—to know—that *purpose* and *human connections* constitute the very heart of business. And I believe they should be at the heart of the necessary and urgent refoundation of business now under way. Capitalism as we have known it for the past few decades is in crisis. More and more people hold the system responsible for social fractures and environmental degradation. Employees, customers, and even shareholders expect much more from corporations than a blind pursuit of profit. Disengagement at work is a global epidemic. More recently, a new civil rights movement and the Covid-19 pandemic have accelerated the need to rethink our system if we want to tackle the enormous challenges facing us.

Business can be a force for good in this fight; it is uniquely positioned to help address some of the world's most pressing issues. A growing number of business leaders agree. But they and I know from experience that it is hard to do.

This is why, as I start the next chapter of my life, I want to share what I have learned over the years. As CEO, I deliberately kept a low profile, politely turning down most requests to appear on TV shows and on the covers of magazines. For me, management is not about the fame and glory of the CEO. It's about the work, and the people I was there to lead and to inspire. Now that I have stepped down, however,

I want to use my energy and my experience to help advance that vision and make it a reality in more places. I want to contribute to the necessary refoundation of business around purpose and humanity.

My beliefs are the culmination of 30 years of reflection, learning, and practice. On my personal journey, I have drawn ideas, knowledge, and inspiration from the work of great thinkers, researchers, and practitioners. These beliefs are therefore grounded in research, spiritual exploration, and the wisdom of others. But I have also formed and tested these beliefs in real life through the transformation of the companies I have led. I have observed and learned from expected and unexpected sources, including great leaders, colleagues, mentors, coaches, family, and friends, as well as French comic books and many popular movies. This book reflects that the leader I have become is an amassing and meshing of thousands of ideas from thousands of places. That is how it *really works*. The notion of the born leader, the superhero with innate abilities, is a myth. What is real is an executive coach pointing out your flaws, or a colleague pointing out a truth so clearly and succinctly you never forget it, or a frontline employee showing you how much you have to learn about the lives of people not like you. Stories like these are found throughout the book because they are what made me the leader I have become, and they are a significant part of what I have to share.

Although this book draws on my experience, it is not a memoir. Neither is it the play-by-play account of the turnaround and transformation of Best Buy or any of the other companies I have led—though those stories will be found throughout. This book is the articulation of key leadership principles for the next era of capitalism, and how to put them into practice in both the best and hardest of times. Throughout the book, these principles are distilled from my own journey, reading, and experience—at Best Buy and elsewhere—rather than laid out as a list.

These key leadership principles and their application unfold in the four parts of this book. Changing the way we approach business starts with changing the way we consider the nature of work. **Part one offers a far more inspiring and positive alternative to the traditional notion of work.** Work is not a curse or something you do so that you can do something else; it can be part of our search for meaning and our fulfillment as human beings.

Part two examines why the traditional view that the primary purpose of business is to maximize shareholder value is wrong, dangerous, and ill-suited to today's environment. Instead, the purpose of a company has to be to contribute to the common good and serve *all* its stakeholders in a harmonious fashion. In order to do so, companies must be viewed as human organizations made of individuals working together in support of an inspiring common purpose—what Lisa Earle McLeod calls a "noble purpose."[1] In the architecture of a new approach to business, a noble purpose is the raison d'être of corporations, and people are at the center of everything they do.

After repositioning the purpose of work and the role and nature of companies, we present in **Part three the very human dimension that powers this architecture and how to unleash what I call *human magic*.** This requires creating an environment that can energize each individual working at the company and results in performance so extraordinary I like to call it *irrational performance*.

Finally, **Part four details the qualities of leadership needed to pull all this together**—the five "Be's" of the purposeful leader. Today's leaders have to be purposeful, be clear about who they serve, be conscious of what their true role is, be driven by values, and be authentic.

If the excessive pursuit of profit as the main objective of business has left you disenchanted or uninspired, this book is for you. If you are looking for an alternative approach to help make business a genuine force for good, this book is for you. If you seek to lead—at any level—with a sense of purpose and humanity to generate extraordinary performance that benefits all stakeholders, this book is for you.

And if you want to understand better how purpose and human connections lead to a long-term success that defies rational expectations, this book is for you.

My hope is that this book will help leaders across all levels of corporations—and anyone trying to live a meaningful, impactful, and joyful life in the world of business—in their journey to become more effective leaders. My hope is that this book will help make business and the world better places.

Part One

THE MEANING OF WORK

W hy do we work? For power? Fame? Glory? Money? Or is it to be useful? To make a difference in the world? Or because we have to, so that we can do something else? How we each answer this question influences our attitude toward work and how invested we are willing to be. Work can be part of our search for meaning and our fulfillment as human beings. If we each shift the way we consider the nature of work, from a burden to an opportunity, then we can start transforming business.

1

Adam's Curse

Work is a necessary evil to be avoided.

—Mark Twain

In June 2012, shortly after I told Jim Citrin he was crazy but before I was invited to become the next CEO of Best Buy, I went to a Best Buy store in Edina, a suburb of Minneapolis. Being a mystery shopper was part of my due diligence on the company. There is no better way to take the temperature of an ailing retailer than to visit a store and buy something.

As soon as I walked through the doors, I found myself in an uninspiring, dark, deserted cave. There were few shoppers. I wandered around the dusty aisles, left alone. I eventually came across three or four sales associates wearing the distinctive Best Buy blue shirts. They were busy talking to each other, uninterested in finding out what I might be looking for and how they might assist me.

I had decided that my shopping experience would be to buy a screen protector for my phone. I find these things hard to put on, and always think I will botch it. So, I grabbed one from a shelf and approached the Blue Shirts, interrupting their conversation to ask whether they would install it for me. Yes, they said without much energy. They would do it. For $18.

I was aghast. $18? Really? I might as well have saved myself the hassle and the money and bought my screen protector online.

I figured the sales associates' approach was company policy. I could easily imagine them being told that they needed to make money off every customer and make sure they could exploit any possible angle to collect dollars.

For me, the mystery shopping experience was a bust. The level of disengagement from the sales associates was striking. They were going through the motions, doing the bare minimum, responding to my queries only when prompted. They clearly had no interest in starting some kind of meaningful conversation with me to explore what else I might need. The simple transaction of buying a screen protector and having it installed felt like pulling teeth. Yes, they had helped me, but I could tell their work brought them no joy, and their attitude and the way they did their work certainly did not inspire me, their customer.

A few days later, I visited another store next to the Best Buy head-quarters in Richfield. This time, I would buy a mobile phone. Immediately, I was encouraged: the store was brighter and did not feel dusty. Even better, I found an LG flip phone going for the princely sum of zero dollars. (This was back when retailers got bounties from phone carriers for getting people on their plans, so they used free phones as an incentive.) The mobile department staff was friendly. After asking for the sales associate to activate the service, including international calls, I left the store, happy. Perhaps my experience at the Edina store had been an unfortunate exception?

But that afternoon, I tried to call my daughter in France using my brand new phone. No luck. The phone did not allow me to make in-ternational calls. This led me into the Kafkian world of customer ser-vice. I first called the store and asked to be connected with the mobile phone department. No one picked up. I then tried the call center and talked to a representative, who could not help me. I eventually had to take another trip to the store to get this fixed. For me, it was a text-book case of a company that had become more focused on selling a product than genuinely seeking to help its customers.

The company was shooting itself in both feet by having front liners no longer able or motivated to truly engage with customers and meet their needs.

Disengagement at Work Is a Global Epidemic

Unfortunately, the Best Buy Blue Shirts I met during my mystery shopper experiment in 2012 are hardly alone. Most people around the world feel indifferent—at best—when it comes to the work they do or the company they work for. Their job does not energize them, and as a result, they are not driven to give their best efforts, energy, attention, or creativity. The ADP Research Institute set out to put an exact number on this global epidemic by surveying over 19,000 workers in 19 countries around the world. They found that only 16 percent of people are "fully engaged" at work. This means more than 8 out of 10 workers merely show up for work—a staggering number. Although levels of disengagement vary from country to country, this is clearly a worldwide phenomenon.[1]

This is a tragedy of unfulfilled personal potential, for we spend a significant part of our lives at work. So much talent and drive are left untapped. Millions of people are denied the chance to be inspired at work, thrive, and be their very best.

This is also a tragedy of unfulfilled economic potential, for study after study confirms how engagement positively influences productivity, reduces employee turnover, increases customer satisfaction and profitability, and even reduces workplace injuries. This disengagement epidemic has been estimated to cost a hefty $7 trillion in lost productivity.[2] Like the Best Buy employees I met at the Edina store, most people clock up for work and get by, dispensing only a fraction of their energy, creativity, brain power, and emotions.

I know the feeling. When I was a teenager, I got a summer job as an assistant mechanic in the body shop of a BMW dealership in my hometown in France. My mechanical skills are limited at best, and I had no interest or real skill for the job. I just needed to make some money. The days were long and dull. I was unable—and to be honest, probably unwilling—to do anything useful at the body shop. The highlight of my day was to take the garbage out, because I could step away from the shop and take more time than necessary to go back. I was a slacker, hiding from work.

After a couple of weeks, I got fired—an inauspicious start to my working life.

The following summer was hardly better. By then, I needed a new bike. And to buy a new bike, I needed money. Work, once again, was a means to an end. A necessary evil. I worked in a grocery store not far from home. All day long, I stuck price tags on vegetable cans for minimum wage. One by one, I took cans out of boxes and hit each one with my tag gun before placing it on the shelf next to the previous one. Again. And again. And again. Green beans. Corn. Tomatoes. I felt every minute of every hour stretch to a standstill. I had no contact with customers, who floated along the self-service aisles. My only human interactions were with colleagues doing similar mindless tasks, and they were just as miserable and withdrawn as I was. There was no coaching of any kind—in any case, I hardly ever saw any manager, let alone talked to one. There was no soul. My only purpose was to earn a few hundred French francs so I could buy myself that new bike and get out the door as fast as I could.

Then I got lucky: I was hit by a truck. I was bringing boxes to be compacted at the back of the store when a fighter jet flew over. A forklift driver got distracted and backed up straight into me. A bruised tailbone got me paid sick leave until the end of the summer, and I eventually got my bike by staying at home doing nothing. Goodbye canned vegetables! I was very happy.

To this day, I recall thinking while I was laid up that I would one day get to manage people. And I pledged to myself that, when that time came, I would remember what it felt like to work a job like this. The emptiness and the sense of disconnection. The indifference toward the company and whether it did well. The meaningless, mind-numbing tasks. Being so disengaged that I would take extra time to empty the trash or relish getting hit by a forklift because it meant getting away from work. I also promised myself that I would then do everything I could so that people who did work such frontline jobs would not feel the same way.

Imagine what would become possible if, instead of less than 20 percent, more than 80 percent of people gave their very best. Business units that top engagement charts are 17 percent more productive and 21 percent more profitable that those that languish at the bottom.[3] Multiple studies have confirmed that more engaged, happier employees directly reflect on the bottom line and on stock price.[4,5]

Besides being more productive and treating customers, colleagues, and suppliers better, people who report being fully engaged at work are also 12 times less likely to quit their jobs.[6] This is true across industries and roles.[7] Employees fired up about work are also 25 to 50 percent less likely to get injured.[8]

If so much good comes from engagement, what explains the global disengagement? It starts with how we view work itself.

Work as a Burden

Traditionally, work is viewed as a chore, a curse, or a punishment even. At best, work is a means to an end—something you do so that you can do something else. You make some money so you can pay the bills, go on holidays, and retire.

When I was president of Electronic Data Systems (EDS) France, I experienced the practical consequences of this perspective. The company was in charge of the technology systems for the 1998 soccer World Cup in France, from ticketing and badges to TV broadcasting and security. We had a team of 80 working on the project. Everyone on that team was fired up, keen to make sure that billions of people would get to enjoy the World Cup in person and on TV. It was a big project: a year before the actual World Cup, we tested our system during a smaller soccer tournament, also hosted in France. Knowing it was a dry run for the big tournament the following year, our team of systems engineers worked 51 hours that week to get it right. In France, however, 51 hours is over the legal limit of weekly work hours. Even if it is just one week, even when it comes to soccer—it is illegal. These laws were meant to protect against overwork in a more industrial age when work was more physically taxing, but the laws remain because work is still viewed as difficult and painful—a burden. As the president of the company, I was personally responsible, and I had to pay a fine.

The concept of work as a curse dates as far back as Greek antiquity, goes all the way to the Industrial Revolution and still impacts how society tends to think and feel about work today. It may have started with Zeus punishing Sisyphus to an eternity of pointless labor, pushing a large boulder up a steep hill just to watch it roll back down. Ancient Greeks viewed work as demeaning, getting in the way of the ideal of a life dedicated to contemplation and the acquisition of knowledge.[9] Romans took a similar view.[10] And the French word for work—*travail*— comes from a Latin word for a torture device.

Christianity's view of work is not any rosier. Exile from Eden and a life of hard labor were Adam's curse for disobeying God's order not to eat from the tree of the knowledge of good and evil.[11] And Eve? She was punished as well, but to painful childbirth—or labor.

The Industrial Revolution brought a new way of working—and new forms of hardship. Work was long, tough, and painful. Think of coal miners working backbreaking shifts, breathing coal dust, and risking explosions. Or textile workers losing fingers in mechanical weaving machines. People worked 14 to 16 hours a day, six days a week, for little pay and no time off. They died young. Although economist Adam Smith viewed labor as the ultimate source of economic wealth for nations, his conclusions on what that meant for the working man (Adam Smith did not seem to think much of working women) were pretty dismal, leading to "the torpor of his mind."[12] In short, work was good for the collective, but terrible for individuals.

Then Frederick Taylor, a young foreman in a steel company, set out to discover, by observing how steel plates were being made, how workers could produce armored steel faster. While more efficient, industrial work became a mind-numbing affair, and workers were reduced to being faceless parts of an all-consuming machine.

This is the vision of industrial work depicted in Charlie Chaplin's 1933 *Modern Times*, in which his character starts off working on an assembly line, screwing nuts faster and faster—until he breaks down and gets swallowed in the cogs of a giant machine. Taylor himself realized that workers performing repetitive tasks were unmotivated and disengaged, doing as little work as they could get away with. And of course, Karl Marx felt that when individuals are denied control over what they produce and how they produce it, they become alienated from their essential human nature.

Objectively, it is easy to see why work has not been viewed as a good thing.[13] In this commonly held view, work is something one does to support one's real life, which occurs when the workday or workweek is over. Not much fun!

A New World—and a Persistent Problem

Now our economic environment—and therefore the nature of work—is going through a radical transformation across the world. Call it a fourth revolution or, like General Stanley McChrystal, a VUCA world: volatile, unpredictable, complex, and ambiguous.[14] Because of fast-changing technology and evolving social norms, agility, innovation, collaboration, and speed have become more valuable than standardized processes and long-term planning.

As a result, the nature of work has changed. The health-damaging physical strain, the Charlie Chaplin kind of mind-numbing repetition, the forklifts running over you, all are declining, as routine tasks get automated. Take my old supermarket summer job. It is being replaced by electronic shelf labels, which get updated at the flick of a finger on a central computer. Even in manufacturing, farming, and other traditionally strenuous occupations, work is becoming less physically demanding. Economies increasingly tilt toward services and more creative work. Two-thirds of all jobs in the US economy now require post-secondary education—up from just 28 percent in 1973—with leadership, communications, and analysis the most valued competencies.[15]

Yet although the nature of work has evolved rapidly, our view of work remains stubbornly unchanged. It is still often considered, if not strictly a curse, then a necessary evil. To some extent, what you do during your workday influences how you feel about work: I felt far more engaged later in my career than when I was sticking price tags on vegetable cans. Senior executives and other knowledge-based professionals report being more engaged than, say, assembly-line workers. Yet the nature of the job itself does not influence how invested people feel in their work as much as one might expect. Less than a quarter of C-suite or VP-level executives are fully engaged in the work they do—not vastly different from other jobs. And there is very little difference across generations: Millennials are not significantly more or less engaged than baby boomers.[16] This leaves enormous room for improvement at all levels, and I believe that people can be invested in their work across all types of jobs.

. . .

In 2019, I was invited to speak at a G100 Network meeting of senior executives. During the event, one participant shared with me how shopping at Best Buy used to leave him utterly frustrated. His experience mirrored my own mystery shopper adventure back in 2012. But then he told me how shocked he had been after a recent trip to a Best Buy store: he had found Blue Shirts genuinely interested in figuring out how to best help him and in providing a great service and experience.

How had we pulled this off? he wanted to know. Had Best Buy changed the entire sales force? Recruited new types of people with a customer service gene? Or concocted a better system of incentives perhaps?

My answers to him were simple: no, no, and no. There had been no forced exodus of store associates, and we had not uncovered any miraculous incentive formula. Natural turnover excepted, these were the same people.

What we did to change his and every other customer's shopping experience was unleash the enormous potential that lies dormant when people merely show up for work or are actively hating their jobs. What we did is turn a large number of disengaged people into engaged employees, inspired to care for their customers.

How?

This is what the rest of this book is about. And it all starts with how we each see work, as well as the human beings doing the work.

Questions to Reflect On

- Have you ever felt that work was boring and not exciting?

- When was that?

- Why was that?

2

Why We Work

Work is love made visible.

—Gibran Khalil Gibran, "On Work"

Imagine this scenario: Jordan is a three-year-old whose favorite toy is a *T. rex* he got for Christmas. Unfortunately, the *T. rex*'s head broke, and the little boy is devastated. He is in tears, and his mom brings him to the local big box store—where, unbeknownst to Jordan, Santa Claus sourced the original *T. rex*. Jordan's mom explains the situation to two sales associates.

Unengaged sales associates will direct Jordan's mom to the toy shelves and let her find a replacement. At best, Jordan gets a new *T. rex* out of it, but he has to throw his beloved old toy into the trash. The sales associates are relieved to see him leave the store and look forward to the end of their workday.

This would be typical, but what if there is an alternative approach? What if we choose to view work not as a curse but in a radically different light? And what if the choice we make between these two visions greatly influences how we engage with work?

We can choose to treat work as what I feel it is: an essential element of our humanity, a key to our search for meaning as individuals, and a way to find fulfillment in our life. Like poet Khalil Gibran eloquently said in a poem dedicated to work, I believe that work is love made visible.

> "Always you have been told that work is a curse and labour a misfortune.
>
> But I say to you that when you work you fulfill a part of earth's furthest dream, assigned to you when that dream was born,
>
> And in keeping yourself with labour you are in truth loving life,
>
> And to love life through labour is to be intimate with life's inmost secret."[1]

This perspective has shaped how I approach my own work. As CEO, it was also my job to encourage every individual at Best Buy to reflect on how they approach theirs.

Work Is Part of Man's Search for Meaning

I have not always considered work in this positive light. My perspective started changing in the early 1990s, when two friends of mine asked whether I would write with them journal articles dealing with the philosophy and theology of work. This was a topic of great interest to me, so I said yes.

I started with research. What did the Bible have to say about work? These were pre-internet days, so I turned to a biblical index, which conveniently listed all the sections of the Old and New Testaments that talk about work. Some, of course, I knew: humans got punished for messing up in paradise: Adam's curse. But having not previously read the Bible cover to cover—and certainly not with this angle in mind!—what I found surprised me.

Most passages shed a light on work completely different from the curse narrative. Story after story dealt with a central question: Why do we work? And for the most part, the answer had nothing to do with sin and penance. Instead, work was portrayed in a far more positive light, and my research led me to a conclusion I did not expect: work is a fundamental element of what makes us human.

This was such a joyous discovery. Like most people—at least most people growing up in Europe—I had been influenced by the deeply rooted collective perspective that work is a bad thing to be endured by the unfortunate who have to make ends meet, and to be avoided by the lucky few who can afford to do so. It is hard to escape centuries-old traditions that permeate our social fabric. Instead, my research was revealing another perspective: a positive, uplifting take on work that spoke to the essence of who we are as human beings. Yes, Adam and Eve got punished for the original sin. But work itself was not the punishment. Pain was. That punishment, unpleasant as it was, did not fundamentally change the nature of work as an essential element of our humanity.

I saw this theme over and over. According to Genesis, God himself worked for six days to create heaven and earth. Then he gave man dominion over the earth, plants and animals included, so humans could make it flourish. This is why Adam was indeed working in paradise: "to cultivate and care for it."[2] Importantly, I read that fulfillment from work comes from doing good things for others—and in so doing, contributing to the common good. Also, work is portrayed as carrying a deeply spiritual meaning rather than something we do to fulfill basic needs.

Having been raised Catholic, I had been exposed to the "social teachings" of the Catholic Church. Beginning in the second half of the nineteenth century, the Church started to articulate its point of view on "Rerum Novarum," these "new things" associated with economic development.[3] These writings confirmed the position that work defines our very humanity. Pope John Paul II wrote, "Human work not only proceeds from the person, but it is also essentially ordered to and has its final goal in the human person."[4]

Through my ongoing exploration and during my travels, I learned that this positive, spiritual, and humanistic perspective was not limited to Catholicism, nor to Christianity, for that matter. Protestant Reformers, for example, embraced work as a source of joy and fulfillment, turning the view of work on its head after centuries of disdain for productive and manual work. For Martin Luther and John Calvin, all productive work—and not just spiritual or religious endeavors—should be viewed as a vocation or calling, a way to serve God and society[5] and to exercise one's God-given talents. Other religions too generally see work as a way to benefit not only oneself, but others as well. Some interpretations of Islam, for example, consider work as service to others, beyond serving individual needs.[6] Similarly, Hinduism embraces the notion of work as service.[7]

The Protestant tradition's enthusiasm about work, for example, struck me when I first moved to the United States in 1985. Then a consultant working for McKinsey & Company, I transferred from Paris to the firm's office in San Francisco, where I discovered a positive mindset and energy. The professionals I met, from entrepreneurs in Silicon Valley to medical researchers and academics at Stanford or Berkeley, spoke passionately about their jobs. Rather than bemoaning challenges, they were excited to find new problems to solve, which they embraced as opportunities. Work wasn't to be endured; it was a good thing, a way to flex one's intellect and creativity. It was an instrument in the "pursuit of happiness." It was the very essence of the American Dream.

Over time, I discovered that this positive view of work is not limited to religion. Sociologists also consider work an essential part of our humanity. Most of us cannot exist without human connections—this is why solitary confinement is considered a form of torture—and work is a way to nurture these connections. Through work, we are part of a web of human interactions, dealing with colleagues, customers, suppliers, and so on. Losing a job is hard—job loss has been shown to be more distressing than divorce[8]—not just because of the economic and financial hardship it creates, but also because it affects our sense of self-worth and, critically, cuts us off from that network of social connections.

Human psychology also sheds a positive light on work. One of the most powerful books I have ever read is Viktor Frankl's *Man's Search for Meaning*. Frankl, an Austrian psychiatrist who was Jewish, survived several concentration camps during the Second World War. His pregnant wife did not; neither did his parents nor his brother. He discovered that those who somehow managed to find meaning in their terrible experience and suffering had a better chance of surviving. To help himself stay alive, Frankl summoned thoughts of his wife and dreams of lecturing after the war about what he was learning in the camps about psychology.

Life, he concluded, is not a quest for pleasure or for power. It is instead a quest for meaning, which ultimately is the path to fulfillment and happiness. And according to him, one can find meaning in three possible places: work, love, and courage. In truth, they often converge; doing something significant through work often involves caring for others and overcoming adversity.

The importance of work as part of our search for meaning is not just an abstract thought. When I was leading Carlson Wagonlit Travel, which provides travel management services to corporations, I experienced firsthand how universal the idea of work as a service to others actually is. There, I saw how teams made of people from around the world, including from countries that have historically fought each other (think of India, China, Japan, Russia, Poland, France, Germany), would coalesce and beautifully work together in service of our global clients such as Accenture, Alcatel, or General Electric.

That search also transcends generations. When asked what would be extremely or very important to them as adults, 95 percent of teens surveyed by the Pew Research Center picked having a job or career they enjoy, which ranked ahead of anything else, including helping people in need, having a lot of money, or having children.[9] A Gallup survey confirmed that finding purpose at work matters deeply to Millennials.[10]

This phenomenon goes way beyond the younger generations and also applies to those of us who are a bit older. Author David Brooks argues that life is often shaped like two mountains: early in their professional life, people chase professional and financial success as well as personal happiness—the first mountain—only to feel unsatisfied once they reach the summit. Later in life, they then embark on a second climb: one focused on finding meaning and purpose through commitment to family, vocation, philosophy or faith, and community.[11]

Back in 2004, it felt like I had reached the top of my "first mountain." My career was going well. I had spent several successful years at McKinsey & Company as a consultant and then a partner. After I decided to move from advising to being responsible for a business, I had led turnarounds at a couple of companies—EDS's French business and the video games division of Vivendi. I had been part of the executive team that restructured Vivendi. I was in my early forties, and I could pride myself with a degree of professional accomplishment. Yet the top of that mountain did feel desolate. The idea of success I had been chasing turned out to be hollow, and I felt disillusioned and empty. I was also struggling in my marriage. I felt I needed to step back and spend time looking into my soul to find a better direction for my life.

Discovering Our Purpose

By some wonderful coincidence, a former client of mine invited me to embark with a handful of other senior executives on the spiritual exercises of Ignatius de Loyola, the founder of the Jesuit order. We spread what is typically a four-week intensive process over two years. The exercises, rooted in contemplation, self-examination, and daily practice under the guidance of a spiritual director, have inspired many other religious orders as well as psychologists' and coaches' practices. The exercises helped me rediscover what was important and, over time, crystallize my calling in life as making a positive difference for people around me and using the platform I have to make a positive difference in the world. Refining this chosen purpose and staying connected to it is a daily practice that continues to this day.

There are multiple ways to travel that journey and discover your purpose. Here are a few that I find particularly effective. In *Discover Your True North*, Bill George highlights the importance of *crucibles* in defining what one's life purpose is going to be.[12] In her book *Aligned*, executive coach Hortense le Gentil shares a range of techniques she uses with her clients, from writing one's own eulogy and revisiting childhood dreams to understanding what gives you energy.[13]

Another useful technique is author Andrés Zuzunaga's approach of finding your purpose at the convergence of four elements: what you love, what you are good at, what the world needs, and what you can get paid for (see the figure below). This is often—albeit inaccurately—believed to represent the Japanese concept of *Ikigai*, which instead is about finding value in daily life.

Whatever tool you use, the goal remains the same: find what gives you energy, what drives you, what you truly and profoundly aspire to, and what stands the test of time.

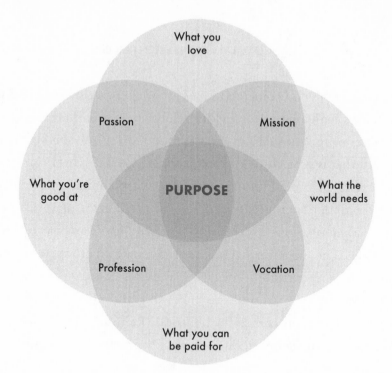

A few words of caution while exploring your purpose: there are potential pitfalls.

Pitfall 1: My purpose will become clear as part of a sudden revelation. The quest for meaning is best approached as a work in progress. We long to find *the* one—*the* dream job that will answer our search for purpose and offer a promise of happily ever after.[14] More often than not, no such Prince or Princess Charming will just show up. I was well into my forties and years into exploring my purpose when I landed on a robust formulation.

Pitfall 2: Purpose must entail intrinsically noble activities. If true, all of us would need to work for a charity or in health care to find purpose and meaning in our life. No doubt these can provide striking examples of purpose. Take GreatCall, a company that Best Buy acquired in 2018 that helps keep seniors living at home by monitoring their health remotely via sensors around their house. The service relies heavily on highly skilled care agents who can provide assistance in case of an emergency. If sensors reveal, for example, that the fridge does not get opened often enough or that people do not get out of bed, the agents can initiate help. When we started investigating GreatCall as a business, we were shocked to learn that fewer than 2 percent of the call agents leave their job every year. In most call centers, turnover is typically over 100 percent a year. It is a draining job to answer customers' complaints and often be unable to help much. GreatCall is a jaw-dropping exception because employees know they are saving lives.

Still, finding meaning and purpose is not restricted to jobs that involve saving lives. It applies to all kinds of work. Easy to say when you have a comfortable, well-paid white-collar job, you might think. But I believe that choice is true at all levels. I love the story of two masons during the Middle Ages, performing the exact same tasks, who were asked about their work. "Don't you see? I'm cutting stones," said the first one, whereas the second took an entirely different view. "I'm building a cathedral," he replied. We get to choose our purpose, and we get to consider how our work is connected to that purpose, regardless of what we do for a living. Like the first mason, zookeepers, for example, could consider their work as dull and boring, or even dirty—zookeepers, four out of five of whom have a college degree, spend a significant part of their day cleaning feces, scrubbing floors, and feeding animals. Instead, few ever quit, because most zookeepers choose to view their work as a personal calling to care for animals.[15] And they are happier for it. The overwhelming majority of zookeepers were found to be willing to sacrifice pay, free time, advancement, and comfort—not that purpose should become an excuse for overwork and underpay.

Even a small dose of meaning makes a difference to engagement. Dan Ariely, professor of psychology and behavioral economics at Duke University, conducted an experiment with Legos. Two groups were asked to build a Lego toy for three dollars, then build another one for thirty cents less, and then another one for still less money. And so on. The Lego constructions of each individual in the first group were placed under the table. The work of the people in the second group, however, was broken in front of their eyes as they were busy building their next Bionicle. Can you guess what happened? People in the second group stopped building toys long before individuals whose work was kept intact.[16]

Pitfall 3: My purpose needs to be big and wide ranging. The idea of purpose can feel daunting and overwhelming. How big should your purpose be? How ambitious? How profound? Although finding meaning and purpose does require introspection and self-awareness, it does not mean retiring to an ashram or a monastery. You do not have to cure cancer either. "Keep it simple," my spiritual director advised me when I was going through my own journey. So as I seek to make a positive difference, it starts with the people around me. With a little help, all of us can find a sense of purpose wherever we are. Start with what gives you energy and joy—in short, what drives you?

Bringing the Purpose Question to Work

"What drives you?" is not a question that gets asked often in corporate environments. Asking it more would be useful, as it can help us connect with a purpose, which in turn determines how we relate to our work. This is why Best Buy employees are encouraged to reflect on that question. "What drives you?" has become a central element of the Best Buy Holiday Leadership Meeting, which gathers some 2,000 managers to kick off the holiday shopping season. I always find the simplicity and humanity of the answers striking. Often, managers talk about friends, family, and colleagues. For a market retail field trainer, it is "being able to see the corners of the world with Grandma Shirley, my favorite person on this planet." For a district manager, it is "helping employees and customers fulfill their hopes and dreams." For a senior HR manager: "teaching, developing, growing and inspiring [people] to do more than they ever thought possible." Encouraging and inspiring everyone at Best Buy to reflect on what drives them may seem a small and woolly step, but it truly has been central to changing how we approach our work.

Understanding your own purpose is one thing. It's just as critical for leaders to understand what drives the individuals around them— and, as we explore in a later chapter, how it connects to the purpose of the organization. To find out what drove each member of Best Buy's executive team, I organized a dinner in 2016, in a room overlooking Minneapolis's beautiful Lake Bde Maka Ska. It was part of one of our regular quarterly retreats. Everyone had been asked to bring pictures of themselves as babies or young children, and to tell a personal story about that picture and about growing up.

Earlier in the day, we had explored the notion of being "all in." Being all in, I figured, has to connect with who we are and who we want to be. So, I wanted to understand what drove each member of our team and how it fit in their lives and their histories. Where did they come from? Why were they excited to work at Best Buy? How did their personal purpose connect with what they were doing at work? I did not feel I could lead our team if I could not answer these questions.

What might sound like a warm and fuzzy game became one of the most memorable and inspiring moments of my time at Best Buy. We truly connected with each other, as the 10 of us took turns talking about what gave us energy and what gave our lives a sense of purpose.

I was moved while listening to each of them describe what drove them personally, from treasuring relationships through unconditional love, infinite support, and the constant fostering of growth, to watching colleagues grow beyond their own expectations by helping them do new things and take on more responsibility.

As inspiring as it was, it was also *useful*. For it made a huge difference in helping us shape our ambitious and meaningful purpose for Best Buy, a purpose that would drive our sustained success in the following years. More to come on this in later chapters.

. . .

Let's think back to Jordan and his broken *T. rex* toy. This is not an imaginary scenario. Jordan and his mom are real people who visited a Best Buy store in Florida in 2019. But the two sales associates did not blankly direct Jordan's mom to a shelf or just hand over a new boxed toy. Instead, they turned into doctors who immediately took the broken dinosaur in for "surgery" behind the counter, where they discreetly exchanged it for a new one while narrating to Jordan the life-saving procedure that was being performed on his "dino baby." After a few minutes of narrating the rescue, they handed over the "cured" dinosaur to a beaming, excited Jordan. For the two Best Buy associates, work was not about collecting a paycheck. It was not about selling a new toy. It was about putting a grin back on a little boy's face.

Applying this very human sense of purpose to work changes how we approach it and therefore how much we engage in it. Does it make work always easy and always fun? No. Everyone has bad days. Every job comes with its challenges. A personal sense of purpose is not in and of itself the only thing that fires people up at work, which is why this book has more than two chapters. But being able to connect what we do every day with a bigger sense of why we do it helps infuse us with energy, drive, and direction. And this is a good start—whether you are a mason, a zookeeper, a Blue Shirt, or a CEO.

Questions to Reflect On

- What drives you?

- What "cathedral" do you want to build?

- What would you like to see included in your eulogy?

- What is at the intersection of what you love, what you are good at, what the world needs, and what you can get paid for?

3

The Problem with Perfection

Perfection does not exist. To understand it is the triumph of human intelligence; the desire to possess it is the most dangerous kind of madness.

—Alfred de Musset, *Confession of a Child of the Century*

"The quest for perfection can be evil!" said Father Samuel.

The two of us were in my office at Carlson Wagonlit Travel in Paris. A few months earlier, I had asked Father Samuel to support a small group of senior executives getting together to reflect on economic and social matters through a spiritual lens. That day in my office, Father Samuel and I were preparing the next session. I do not remember the details of what we were discussing. But to this day, I still remember his exact words on perfection, and the profound—and lasting—impact they had on me.

"What do you mean?" I asked him.

Samuel's point was deeply spiritual. He explained how God's favorite angel one day decided that he was complete and perfect—the best—which is how he became the devil. "You cannot love others and develop a relationship with them if you do not first accept that you are imperfect and vulnerable, and need help," concluded Father Samuel.

I was stunned, for it went against everything I had been taught. My entire life, I had been driven to excel. My mother, determined to cultivate the potential she saw in me, relentlessly expected me to always do better and go higher, instilling in me a vision of success steeped in perfection and glory. School also trained me to strive for perfection, to be the best and the smartest. All my teachers focused on mistakes and imperfections, attempting to root them out with a red pen. I had been taught to aim for perfect grades. How well I did in high school would then determine higher education opportunities. Entrance exams were based on rankings, which required being better than the next person to get in an elite school. Going to an elite school would in turn influence job opportunities. And in large companies, early success was largely about being smart and not making mistakes. Everything was geared toward making perfection the ideal to strive for.

To my surprise, I found Father Samuel's idea convincing. So did the other CEOs in our study group. Father Samuel's words resonated because we all had to varying degrees approached work as a quest for perfection. All this time, we—I—had been confusing performance and perfection. Aiming for outstanding business performance is a good thing; expecting human perfection is not. Every time I have invited Father Samuel to speak to leaders since then, this is the idea they remember most.

The quest for perfection looms large among the 20 "behavioral quirks" that prevent successful leaders from doing even better, according to my former executive coach Marshall Goldsmith: think of habits such as needing to show people that you are the smartest person in the room, wanting to win in all situations, and systematically inserting yourself whenever a problem needs solving.[1] In fact, when Marshall's clients get together, we often discuss how badly afflicted we each were prior to working with him. "That's nothing—I was much worse!" We are still striving to be the best at being the worst perfectionist.

Although I embraced Father Samuel's words as a brilliant new outlook, it took me years to translate his wisdom into practice. If work is a defining element of our humanity and an answer to our quest for meaning, then how can seeking perfection in that be wrong? Leaving aside the religious notion of "evil," I have learned over time why treating work as a quest for perfection, even in the context of our search for purpose, is counterproductive.

My Struggle with Feedback

For most of my career, I dismissed feedback, especially when it suggested that I had things to work on. Instead, I would spend my energy trying to identify who had said what, and pinpoint what was wrong with *them*.

The first time I got feedback from my team was at McKinsey. By most measures, I was a successful consultant: I had become partner by age 30, significantly younger than most. Things were going well, and I thought I was really good. Then, my team assessed me, noting areas where I was performing above and below average. Of course, I had not expected any below average ratings. But there they were. I was devastated and paralyzed. How was it possible that I had problematic "development needs"? I did not know what to do with that feedback, so I put it aside and did nothing.

Obviously, that would not help me improve, and by the time I became CEO of Carlson Wagonlit Travel in 2004, after successfully working myself out of a job while helping restructure Vivendi, I still struggled with feedback. Once again, everything was going perfectly well from my perspective. We were on our way to tripling the size of the company and quintupling its profitability. We were gaining new customers. The corporate travel industry was in a disruptive transition from a cottage industry of airline agents to a far more sophisticated, tech-driven business whose customers were companies. Having spent years as a management consultant and then at EDS, I felt I knew a lot about everything Carlson Wagonlit needed. I knew about business-to-business services. I knew about IT services. I knew about human resources and how to manage performance. And so, of course, I could make things better!

That was a problem. I thought I had all the answers, so I tended to look at others as obstacles rather than valuable partners, because I focused on their imperfections. I believed I could do it better than they could. Whenever a team would share some proposal or business plan with me, I would make sure to tell them how to improve it. Marshall Goldsmith, I later learned, calls this "adding too much value." Without even realizing it, I was telling my teams what they should do. And for years, I kept trying to solve problems for them. In retrospect, this must have deeply demoralized them.

At the time, I did not see it that way. There were signs, though: at one of the company's parties, the head of CWT Human Resources, who had a good sense of humor, produced an org chart with my name in every box. We had a good laugh, but I was annoyed. Soon after, an even more direct message came from an employee survey, which showed that people reporting directly to me were not very invested in their work. That stung, especially since, as a whole, the company had quite good levels of employee engagement.

I was gripped by what psychologists label cognitive dissonance: I believed I was doing great, yet the data showed I could do better. Cognitive dissonance is so uncomfortable that the typical reaction is to become singularly focused on reconciling the disconnect. Back then, I reconciled it by telling myself there was nothing wrong with me. And if there was nothing wrong with *me*, then the problem had to be *them*.

Why were they not seeing how great I was? And how much I was helping? That was troubling.

It was around that time, while I was still at Carlson Wagonlit Travel,
that I had my discussion with Father Samuel about perfection. I understood his argument and fully agreed with it. But ingrained habits
are hard to change.

My name was Hubert, and I was a perfectionist. I needed help.

Embracing Imperfection

A few years later, when I became the CEO of Carlson Companies, which
owned Carlson Wagonlit Travel and other brands like Radisson Hotels
and TGI Friday's, the head of HR, Elizabeth Bastoni, asked me if
I wanted to work with an executive coach. You will not be surprised to
know that I was reluctant. I had no problem with coaching for my tennis
game or skiing. But my job was another matter. In fact, if you had told
me at that time that a fellow executive was using a coach, I would have
thought, *What is wrong with that person? What problem does he or she have?*

In my defense, executive coaching at the time was perceived as remedial. So why should I get a coach? Elizabeth explained that Marshall
Goldsmith helped successful leaders become even better. His list of clients was impressive. Suddenly, it was as if I had been told: *I see you love
playing tennis and you're good at it. Would you like to continue to improve your
game?*

Of course I wanted to get better! So I started working with Marshall. I learned to look at feedback as "feedforward" and to choose
areas I wanted to work on. It is a subtle but important distinction:
I was not focused on fixing a problem, but rather deciding what
I wanted to get better at. This is how I learned to thank people for
feedback, tell them what I was working on, and ask them for advice.
I learned to check in with them, hear from them how I was doing, and

ask for more advice. I learned to embrace the feedback I used to put aside.

Through the experience of someone close to me who was dealing with depression, I later discovered that psychologists echo Father Samuel's words on perfection, vulnerability, love, and human connections. Perfectionism, it turns out, is not good for you: abundant research has linked it to depression, anxiety, eating disorders, and even suicide.[2]

All those years, I expected others to be impossibly perfect, while ignoring my own vulnerabilities. This severely limits human relationships—and therefore collaboration, effective teamwork, and leadership. Employees are more inspired by vulnerable leaders than leaders who project unreasonable strength and perfection, because we relate and bond through our imperfections. Brené Brown, who defines herself as a "researcher, storyteller, Texan," has spent the past two decades studying vulnerability, courage, shame, and empathy. She explicitly lists connection as one of the gifts of imperfection—along with courage and compassion.[3] What stands in the way of connection, she has found, is shame, or the fear that there is something that, if others see and know about us, will make us unworthy of connection. People who felt a strong sense of love, connection, and belonging, on the other hand, were those who had the courage to be imperfect and who embraced vulnerability.[4] All this taught me that there can be no genuine human connection without vulnerability, and no vulnerability without imperfection.

I have also learned from other business leaders about how the quest for perfection hinders rather than advances great work. Alan Mulally, the former CEO of Ford, was kind enough to share how, early in the company's turnaround, he had encouraged his colleagues to openly admit when and where they had problems.

When Alan became CEO in 2006, Ford was expected to lose $17 billion that year. And it did. As he put it, the company did not have a forecasting problem: it had a performance problem, part of which was a corporate culture in which admitting problems was seen as a sign of weakness. Alan implemented a "traffic lights" color system for reports on key performance areas, which were discussed every Thursday during his Business Plan Review meetings. All the members of the leadership team had to color-code the weekly status report against their teams' goals: green when everything was on track; amber when things were off the rails, but there was a plan to get back on track; and red when performance was off, and the team did not yet have a plan to get back on course.

Alan told us how, in the first few weeks, everything was green. The company was facing a substantial loss, but looking at the charts, everything was going according to plan. "You know, we are losing billions of dollars," Alan pointed out. "Isn't there *anything* that's not going well?" Mark Fields, who would later succeed Alan as CEO, was the first to take a risk and admit that not everything was perfect. He was then in charge of Ford's Americas operations, and he had a problem with the highly anticipated launch of the Ford Edge in Canada: testing had revealed a grinding noise in the suspension that had not yet been resolved, and he had decided to put the launch on hold. At the next weekly meeting, he characterized the launch as red and explained that they had not yet figured out how to solve the problem.

According to Alan, eyes went to the floor, and the air left the room. But Alan began to clap. "Who can help Mark with this?" he asked. Suddenly, someone raised his hand: he would send his quality experts right away. Someone else offered to ask suppliers to check their components. Alan, himself an engineer, did not jump in. He relied on his team to collaborate, rather than insert himself. The problem with the Ford Edge was resolved quickly.

It took a few more weekly meetings, but eventually more red and amber appeared on the charts. By then, everyone on the team trusted that they could openly acknowledge problems and would help each other turn red into amber and then green.

Alan Mulally's story illustrates another problem with the quest for perfection: no one can ever have all the answers. In healthy work environments, no one will be afraid of saying they do not know. Yet as obvious as that sounds, many people still believe that saying "I don't know" is viewed as weakness. I remember as a teenager, one of my parents' friends, who was a businessman, asked me a question. I cannot remember the question, but I remember saying to him: "I don't know."

He looked at me and said: "Young man, I hope you will never say that in the business world, because this is admitting a weakness, and you should never do this. This will limit your potential."

I have wrestled with perfectionism, but even back then, this made no sense to me. If I did not know, well, I did not know! What was wrong with that? I could always learn and find out. I was not pigeonholing myself by saying I am not good at math, or I am not a visual thinker. I was not saying *I cannot know*. I just did not know. If someone asks you about last month's market share or what section 1502 of the Dodd-Frank Act is all about, there is nothing wrong with saying, "I don't know. Let me look into it!"

Alan Mulally thwarted perfectionism so problems could be acknowledged and resolved. Amazon's CEO Jeff Bezos points out that perfectionism also impedes innovation by making us afraid to fail. "I believe we are the best place in the world to fail," he wrote in a letter to shareholders. "Failure and invention are inseparable twins. To invent, you have to experiment, and if you know in advance that it's going to work, it's not an experiment. Most large organizations embrace the idea of invention but are not willing to suffer the string of failed experiments necessary to get there."[5]

Learning about the benefits of imperfection would profoundly transform how I approached my role at Best Buy, and without it, the transformation might not have gone the way it did. We will describe later in this book how, once Best Buy successfully emerged from its turnaround and embarked on a growth strategy, we worked hard to shift a collective mindset away from perfectly hitting targets and toward what Stanford University professor of psychology Carol Dweck defines as a "growth mindset," or the idea that talent and abilities can be developed through effort and learning. Mistakes and failure are essential to learning, but they do not sit well with perfectionism, which is instead associated with a "fixed mindset"—the view that abilities are innate and fixed. Carol Dweck points out that wanting to be seen as perfect is often called the "CEO disease," as it afflicts many leaders.[6] Unfortunately, the need to establish superiority by exhibiting effort-less perfection means there is little incentive to take on anything challenging—and therefore to learn—for fear of failing.

So much of business life is driven by the quest to be "the best" or "number one"—a symptom of Dweck's fixed mindset. Many companies, Best Buy included, have a system of scorecards and rankings to measure and reward performance. Rankings are everywhere. Being the best is even in Best Buy's name. It is a disease—one that, according to psychologists, feeds a growing and self-defeating quest for perfection.[7] The problem is, the idea of being the best implies that the world is a zero-sum game. There is room for only 10 people or companies in the top 10. You can only become number one by knocking off someone else. And then what do you do when you become number one? There is nowhere else to go but down. Of course, there is competition, and competition is important. But competition against oneself, or doing better tomorrow than we did yesterday, takes us much further than obsessively measuring ourselves against others.

We all work—and lead—best when we embrace vulnerability, learn from failure, and strive to be *our* best rather than *the* best. For it is in these imperfections that we can truly and deeply connect with others.

A Strategic Breakthrough

Shortly after I started at Best Buy, I introduced Marshall to my executive team. I would continue the work on letting go of perfectionism. I openly laid out what I wanted to get better at and enrolled the team's help to track my progress.

I still had work to do in one area: my penchant for jumping in where I was not needed. This was clear in 2016, when the executive team worked with leadership coach Eric Pliner on operating more effectively as a team. As we discussed what was standing in our way, someone said that our strategy was not clear enough. Then that idea kept coming up again.

I thought we had a clear growth strategy, called Building the New Blue. Everybody had worked on it; the board had approved it. So, I was surprised—and a little annoyed. I took it personally. It was, after all, my responsibility as CEO to make sure we had a clear strategy and that everyone was on board.

Yet I was being told that Renew Blue, our 2012 turnaround plan that preceded Building the New Blue, was a much clearer strategy. In my mind, Renew Blue was not really a strategy. It had been a set of operational steps to survive and recover.

But my colleagues saw it as a full-on strategy with a crystal-clear message: change or die. Our current strategy, they said, lacked that clarity.

"Let me work on it," I said.

The team's reaction was swift: "No!"

They understood that the issue was that our strategy was not clear *for them*. The answer was not for *me* to jump in and make it clearer. The solution was to create an environment in which the team, and everyone at the company, could participate to ensure they understood and owned it, down to its practical day-to-day implications for their jobs. I did not have to insert myself to solve every problem and make more decisions than I needed to. But my impulse was to try.

Part of our work with Eric Pliner was to clarify who should be responsible for what decisions. We adopted the popular RASCI model, which triages who should be responsible (R), accountable (A), supporting (S), consulted (C), or merely informed (I), according to the situation—something we revisit in more detail in part three.

It was a breakthrough for me—a lightbulb moment. When I had first become CEO and the company was sinking, I made lots of decisions, fast. But now things were going well. We had an extraordinary team of highly talented people who respected and trusted each other. Decisions did not have to be made *by me* all the time. It had taken many years for me to get there, but I was ready to let go of all my inclinations to be perfect. It was liberating, both for me and for the organization. It took the intervention of two coaches, much reading and listening, and years of practice, but I was finally able to put Father Samuel's words into practice.

. . .

Changing how we view work and how we engage with it is a journey of personal transformation, a journey toward embracing work as neither a curse or a chore, nor a quest for perfection, but as a path toward fulfilling our own purpose. It starts with each individual in the company, from front liner to CEO.

Only then are we able to start transforming business and unleashing collective human magic.

Questions to Reflect On

- What are your quirks? How do you find out about them?

- How do you take feedback?

- How do you decide to work on something you want to get better at?

- Have you told your team what you want to work on?

- What help are you getting?

Part Two

THE
PURPOSEFUL
HUMAN
ORGANIZATION

The refoundation of business starts with considering work as an answer to our quest for meaning and fulfillment, as laid out in part one. In part two, we examine why the traditional view that the primary purpose of business is to maximize shareholder value is wrong, dangerous, and ill-suited to today's environment. Contrary to what Milton Friedman wanted us to believe, the purpose of a company is not to make money, but rather to contribute to the common good and serve *all* its stakeholders. And corporations are not soulless entities, but human organizations with people at their center, working together in support of that purpose. This new approach to business does not apply just when everything is going well; it is particularly relevant in challenging times. In fact, this approach underpinned Best Buy's successful turnaround and resurgence.

4

The Tyranny of Shareholder Value

Wealth is evidently not the good we are seeking; for it is merely useful and for the sake of something else.

—Aristotle, *The Nicomachean Ethics*

In December 2019, my children and I got together for the holiday season, as we do every year. The year, and the decade, were coming to a close. Both my son and my daughter were stepping into their thirties and starting their own families; a few months earlier, I had turned 60 and stepped down as CEO at Best Buy. It was a moment of reflection for all of us.

The news also weighed heavily on our minds: catastrophic forest fires were ravaging New South Wales and Victoria in Australia, a few months after raging in Brazil's Amazon and, again, in California. Social fires were burning too. France was gripped by strikes over the government's proposed pension reform, following months of protests initially triggered by a rise in fuel prices. Mass protests had broken out in Lebanon, Chile, Ecuador, Bolivia, and elsewhere. Unrest over the economy and, more generally, growing inequality was feeding a global wave of populism while demands for more action on climate change inspired a rising tide of protests around the world, led by younger generations rallying behind Swedish teenage activist Greta Thunberg.

Around the dinner table, my children talked about how excessive consumerism and waste was contributing to global warming. They pointed out that young professionals in their generation were turning to start-ups in search of inspiration and fulfillment at work because they were disillusioned with large traditional employers. Both felt that governments and business were not doing an adequate job to address the climate crisis, seemingly lacking the sense of urgency that they felt so acutely. What kind of world would they and their children be living in over the decades to come?

One thing was clear to us: our capitalist system and the way business was operating no longer seemed sustainable.

My children are not alone in believing that our economic system has reached an impasse. Multiple surveys have made it clear that social inequality and the environmental crisis are feeding disenchantment with capitalism, especially among younger generations.[1] Of course, capitalism has led to an unprecedented period of economic development, driving extraordinary innovation and taking billions of people out of poverty. But we are undeniably facing a crisis.[2] In fact, in January 2020, Marc Benioff, the outspoken CEO of Salesforce, declared at the annual meeting of the World Economic Forum in Davos, where discussions largely focused on how to address climate change and inequality: "Capitalism as we have known it is dead."

We need to rethink how our economic system works.

One of the first things I learned in business school, back in 1978, was that the purpose of business was to maximize shareholder value, and I believed it. My training focused on acquiring techniques to optimize profits. No time was spent thinking about the role of business in society. The history, philosophy, and ethics I had studied in high school and during my early college years disappeared from the curriculum, and I went straight into double-entry accounting and financial analysis. I clearly remember a strategy game that we played in which winning was entirely based on who made the most profit. I carried this ethos into the early 1990s, when I transferred to the McKinsey office in New York. Despite a decade of financial excess and banking scandals, that view held. As strategy consultants, our objective was generally to maximize shareholder value for our clients.

We largely owe this gospel to Milton Friedman, one of the most influential economists of the twentieth century. In a *New York Times* article published in September 1970, he argued that business has one and only one "social" responsibility: to maximize profits for shareholders. According to Friedman, people who believe that business should not be concerned merely with profits but should also promote social ends such as providing employment or avoiding pollution are preaching pure socialism.[3] Milton Friedman's perspective has one obvious advantage: it is simple. There is just one constituency to please—shareholders—and one performance metric that matters—profits.

The Friedman doctrine remained business gospel for decades. In 1997, the Business Roundtable, which includes the CEOs of the largest and most influential companies in the United States, published a statement that declared: "The Business Roundtable wishes to emphasize that the principal objective of a business enterprise is to generate economic returns to its owners."[4]

My view started changing when I was still a consultant, and my subsequent experience at the helm of several companies only confirmed what I started to feel in those latter days at McKinsey. I now see shareholder primacy as the root cause of the problems that my children and I were talking about around the dinner table. Although making money is of course vital and a natural outcome of good management (as we discuss in chapter 5), considering profit as the sole purpose of business is wrong for four fundamental reasons: (1) profit is not a good measure of economic performance; (2) an exclusive focus on it is dangerous; (3) this singular focus antagonizes customers and employees; and (4) it is not good for the soul.

Profit Is Not a Good Measure of Economic Performance

Profit does not take into account the impact of a business on the rest of society. The full cost of waste or carbon footprint on the environment does not appear on a financial statement, even though it is very real and can be very painful. Food and beverage companies using single-use plastic bottles, for example, do not bear the cost of oceans being clogged up with plastic waste. The profits of businesses relying on coal as their main source of fuel do not reflect the costs they generate on human health and the environment.

Even within the confines of a company's four walls, a company's profit can be a misleading measure of economic performance. I learned just how arbitrary accounting norms can be when, in April 2003, I became the deputy CFO of Vivendi, overseeing the company's financial reporting and planning.

It was a chaotic context. After a string of acquisitions, the group faced a liquidity crunch that had led to the exit of the CEO, Jean-Marie Messier, about nine months earlier. Concurrently, the company's auditors, Arthur Andersen, had collapsed after the Enron scandal. Vivendi had decided to issue a high-yield bond in the United States and in Europe to extend the maturity of its existing debt, so it could sell some of the company's assets without being under cash pressure. We had to close the books in order to be able to market the high-yield bond.

As I worked with the company's new auditors to unpack our financial reporting, I was struck by disconnects between reported earnings and economic reality. For example, according to accounting rules, a parent company can include 100 percent of the operating income of the businesses it controls in its own operating income, even if it owns only a fraction of these businesses. The income of businesses it does not control, on the other hand, is not included at all in that line, even when the parent company owns a significant portion of these businesses. Vivendi had been—somewhat conveniently—consolidating profitable businesses in which it held a minority stake, namely mobile operator SFR (44 percent) and Maroc Telecom (35 percent). At the same time, it was not consolidating unprofitable businesses, such as Polish telecom company PTC and internet platform Vizzavi, even though it owned about 50 percent of each. This was entirely legal and in line with accounting rules, but it inflated Vivendi's operating income and divorced profit from the actual health of the business.

In addition, it is hard to account for other signs of a healthy business, like motivated and skilled people, a company's most important asset. Engaged employees were the engine of Best Buy's successful turnaround and remain the number-one reason for its continued success today. Yet you cannot find them on the balance sheet. As a result, investing in people, like Walmart CEO Doug McMillon decided to do back in 2016, and like we did at Best Buy, can depress profits in the short term, whereas investments in tangible assets such as real estate or plants will be amortized over several years.

A Singular Focus on Profit Is Dangerous

Profit—like the temperature of a patient—is a symptom of other underlying conditions, not the condition itself. And focusing on the symptom alone can be dangerous. Think of a doctor who is rewarded merely for keeping patients' temperature within a healthy range. The thermometer might end up in the fridge whenever a patient runs a fever.

It is an easy game to rig, and not just through accounting. I can maximize profit by underinvesting in people and other assets that directly benefit customers. It works, but for a short time. Expenses go down, and the numbers look good for a time while the long-term health of the business suffers. This is precisely what happened at Best Buy between 2009 and 2012, when the company slowed down spending on its stores and invested too little in e-commerce. At the same time, it increased prices. For a while, that helped sustain its bottom line—until customers grew tired of battling with the company's website, and of the dusty stores and poor customer service I encountered when I went to buy my flip phone. The path to bankruptcy is littered with retailers like Sears and others that focused more on short-term profits than on investing in talent and better serving customers. Best Buy, as the following chapters show, illustrates that focusing on talent and customers is what underpins *sustainable* success.

A relentless focus on just "hitting the numbers" stifles innovation too. A Stanford University study found that innovation at tech companies slows by 40 percent after initial public offerings (IPOs) because management becomes more cautious once they are subject to market pressures.[5]

If you try to manage to a certain number, you also risk missing the opportunity to play offense during downturns. During the 2008 Great Recession, I was at Carlson, and the hospitality industry was severely hit. I could see how the leaders in that industry, Marriott or Starwood, to name a couple, continued to invest even if it meant hurting their profits in the short term.

Of course, financial performance does matter a great deal. Profit creates space and time. Listed companies that don't hit market expectations can quickly lose value. In January 2014, for example, Best Buy's share price dropped from $39 to $25, on the back of disappointing holiday sales numbers. I had to remind myself that, over the previous year, the share price had gone from $11 to $42. Markets react fast—and often overreact in the short term. And in the longer term, a CEO who consistently fails to deliver financial performance will be ousted, and a company that is not profitable is doomed. Whereas such pressures cannot be ignored, they do not justify myopia.

And they certainly do not justify wrongdoing. A steady stream of corporate scandals through the past two decades, such as Enron's house of cards, Volkswagen's "dieselgate," and Wells Fargo's scandal, are direct consequences of an excessive focus on numbers. The 2008 recession was the result of bad behavior on a large scale, demonstrating the danger of this approach to running a business.

A Singular Focus on Profit Antagonizes Customers and Employees

Consumers are smart and demanding. Like my children, they have high expectations of companies. They want to do business with companies they respect and trust to be competent, ethical, and actively improving the society around them.[6] Consumers increasingly will turn away from companies that do not meet these standards. One of the points that my children raised over our dinner was the forced obsolescence of the products they buy, how quickly tech companies stop supporting older products and how often some clothing retailers come up with new lines, a phenomenon known as "fast fashion." They see these tactics as merely a profit strategy, and not beneficial to them or the planet.

Multiple industries, from food to fashion, are feeling the pressure to clean up their climate act. Concerns over global warming are shaping behavior—and consumption. Before Covid-19 devastated air travel, one in five people said they were flying less out of concern over the environment.[7] A "flight shame" movement was spreading beyond Sweden's borders. These trends cannot be ignored.

Employees are also pushing for social and environmental change from their employers. For example, in September 2019, Amazon employees walked out to pressure their employer to be more ambitious about reducing its carbon footprint, stop servicing the oil and gas industry, and no longer support politicians who deny climate change.

Even shareholders—the very people who supposedly benefit the most from the belief that the sole purpose of companies is to make money—are looking beyond short-term profits and increasingly adopting the view that being a good citizen is ultimately good for business. BlackRock, the world's largest asset manager, has embraced sustainability as its new standard for investing. In its 2020 annual letter to CEOs, BlackRock head Larry Fink explained that climate change, in particular, creates investment risks. "Climate change," he wrote, "has become a defining factor in companies' long-term prospects [. . .] Our investment conviction is that sustainability- and climate-integrated portfolios can provide better adjusted-risk returns to investors."[8] Business leaders, nongovernmental organizations (NGOs), and academics surveyed by the World Economic Forum in its 2020 Global Risks Report ranked the failure to mitigate and adapt to climate change as the top threat facing the world over the next 10 years.[9]

Shareholders' expectations are shifting because investors themselves are not soulless entities unable to lift their gaze past the next quarterly results. Shareholders are people or organizations of people—whether institutional investors or mutual funds—that are looking after the financial security and pensions of other people. Either way, they are individuals. And as such, they are not homogeneous; they tend to have varying objectives and time horizons. They are also human beings who share the same planet and the same human aspirations as everybody else, as well as concerns about the future. They are consumers and employees too.[10]

The push from investors away from the primacy of shareholder value is not just in words. Assets invested and managed taking into account environmental, social, and governance criteria rose from $22.8 trillion in 2016 to $30.7 trillion at the beginning of 2018.[11] In addition, climate considerations are increasingly being included in financial reporting, affecting investment decisions.[12] It is not going away. Customers, employees, and even shareholders are resetting expectations.

An Exclusive Focus on Profit Is Not Good for the Soul

In early 1999, when I was president of EDS France, I attended a leadership meeting with the new CEO of the global group, based in Texas. He was presenting the company's strategy. This presentation only strengthened my growing conviction that the Friedman doctrine was wrong. The CEO's entire approach was focused on profit. I felt uninspired. When he asked for feedback, my contribution was to point out that financial results could not be our sole focus. Over the following few months, the new CEO's approach heightened my sense of alienation, which convinced me to leave EDS.

If, when I joined Best Buy in 2012, I had told everyone at the company that our purpose was to double our earnings per share to $5, what do you think would have happened? Not much. And for good reason. When we ask Best Buy employees what drives them, no one ever says "shareholder value." This is not why people jump out of bed in the morning. If we want employees to be more invested, we must acknowledge that their souls are not wrapped up in a stock price. Remember, work does not have to be a chore; it is not a curse. It is a quest for meaning. Maximizing profit does not answer that quest and therefore cannot solve the epidemic of disengagement at work we discussed in part one. It is not what drives people to give their very best to save companies like Best Buy.

I am not for a second suggesting that we should ignore profits. Of course, companies *must* make money—or they do not survive. And there are situations where a keen focus on the bottom line is a good thing. When a business is bleeding money and at risk of dying, for instance, you have to prioritize stopping the hemorrhage. Also, it is healthy to know how and why the business will make money.

But what is healthier still is to disavow the *obsession* with the bottom line. The true bottom line is this: although profit is vital, it is an outcome, not a purpose in itself.

Then, you might ask, if not profit, what is the purpose of a company? Properly framing the answer to this question is how we start reinventing capitalism, transforming business from the inside, and helping to shape our collective future. In so doing, we can begin to answer the aspirations and concerns that my children—and probably yours as well, together with millions of other people—voice around the dinner table.

For me, this journey started in 1993 around a different dinner table, with a business discussion that would start opening my eyes to the true heart of business.

Questions to Reflect On

- Do you believe that the only purpose of companies is to maximize profits, and their primary responsibility is to shareholders? If so why, and if not, why not?

- Do you think that the expectations of your company's customers, employees, and shareholders have changed? And if so, has your company changed with them?

5

The Business of Building Cathedrals

No sire, it's not a revolt; it's a revolution.

—François Alexandre Frédéric de La Rochefoucauld-Liancourt, a French social reformer, to Louis XVI, the morning after the storming of the Bastille in 1789

"The purpose of a corporation is not to make money!" Jean-Marie Descarpentries, the newly appointed CEO of Honeywell Bull, exclaimed. It was 1993, and I was working at McKinsey in Paris. My colleagues and I had invited Descarpentries to dinner to explore how we could help him in his new role. I had my sales hat on, fully expecting to spend the evening understanding his priorities and pitching him.

But instead, Jean-Marie decided to brief us on what had been discussed at a gathering of French CEOs he had recently attended. In his typical animated and passionate way, he shared his views on business and how it was to be conducted.

The purpose of companies was not to make money?

My fork stopped midair. This went against everything I had learned in business school and over my early career as a management consultant. These words squarely contradicted the basic assumptions of mainstream business. What about shareholders? What about Milton Friedman?

Over steak and wine, Jean-Marie clarified what he meant for a roomful of skeptical consultants. He was not suggesting we burn cashflow statements. He was saying that making money is a vital imperative and an outcome for business. But it is not its ultimate goal.

This felt big. I had so far in my career not found the idea of maximizing shareholder value particularly inspiring, but it was just the way things were. This suggested there might be another, more inspiring way. I listened closely. Jean-Marie explained that companies have in fact three imperatives: people, business, and finance.

These three imperatives are *linked*. Excellence on the first imperative—the development and fulfillment of employees—leads to excellence on the second—loyal customers buying your company's products and services again and again. This then leads to excellence on the third imperative, which is making money. The causal link goes like this:

People → Business → Finance

This makes profit an outcome of the first two imperatives. Jean-Marie said there is no real trade-off between these imperatives; the best companies achieve excellence on all three simultaneously.

Yet imperative and outcome, he went on, should not be confused with *purpose*. The company's purpose, he said, is the development and fulfillment of its people, and the attention given to the people around them.

Jean-Marie's energy was contagious, and his ideas struck a deep chord in me. As a management consultant, I knew how much effort was spent on tactics: what products and services to offer; where and how to position oneself to be competitive. Little thought went toward articulating an inspiring *purpose*. Yet this made complete sense to me. And here, finally, was something I could feel inspired about.

That conversation led me to look at business in an exciting and radically new light as I observed Jean-Marie put his principles into practice during our subsequent work together. And when I left consulting, it shaped the way I approached my job as CEO, starting with EDS France and all the way to Best Buy. This chapter discusses this shift in perspective, and chapters 6 and 7 cover its practical implications in greater detail.

Focusing on Purpose and People

As highlighted in chapter 4, we urgently need to reinvent capitalism from the inside out. The good news is, we can.

Over the years, I have developed—and put to the test again and again—an approach that lays out the architecture for a refoundation of business and capitalism. It builds on the wisdom received from Jean-Marie Descarpentries and many others along the way.

This approach is based on a seismic shift from profit to purpose: I believe that business is fundamentally about purpose, people, and human relationships—not profit, at least not primarily. Companies are not soulless entities. They are human organizations made of individuals who work together toward a common purpose. When that common purpose aligns with their own individual searches for meaning, it can unleash a kind of human magic that results in outstanding performance.

The figure below lays it out:

**The purposeful human organization—a declaration
of interdependence**

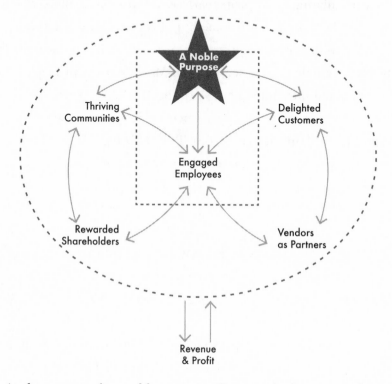

At the very top is a noble purpose. Purpose is the reason the company exists. A noble purpose, a term borrowed from Lisa Earle
McLeod,[1] is the positive impact it is seeking to make on people's lives
and, by extension, its contribution to the common good. That common
good is the core focus of the company and is integrated in every aspect
of what the company does. Business does well by doing good.

Employees—at the center—rally around the noble purpose, and customers profoundly relate to it. It becomes a guiding North Star against
which strategy is formulated and every decision made and measured.

The idea of personal purpose as the intersection of four elements
introduced in chapter 2 is helpful when considering company pur-

pose and how it differs from the narrower ideas of corporate philan-
thropy or corporate social responsibility. A company's reason for being
can also be found in the same way: what the world needs, what we as
a team are passionate about, what the company is good at, *and* what it
can get paid for. This concept has inspired the four questions that
Best Buy uses when considering new business ideas:

- Does it fit with our purpose as a company?

- Is it good for the customer?

- Can we deliver?

- *And* can we make money?

A noble purpose is at the top of my framework. Employees stand at
its center because the secret of business is to have great people do great
work for customers in a way that delivers great results. Employees and
the work they do cannot and should not be considered merely inputs,
as economic theory would have us believe. No one wants to be an input.
Doing great work starts when people feel treated like individuals—not
human capital—in a work environment where they can thrive.

The architecture I am advocating has employees at the heart of business, creating and nurturing caring and authentic relationships both
within the company and also with all of the company's stakeholders—
customers, vendors, local communities, and shareholders—in a way that not
only contributes to the company's purpose but also creates great outcomes for each of these stakeholders. *Doing great work for customers* happens when employees relate to these customers as human beings, not
walking wallets. It happens when employees, from the CEO to front
liners, genuinely understand and care about what customers need
and how they can best help them answer these needs. Delighting customers in this way is how love brands—brands that have built a strong
emotional bond with their customers—are created, inspiring loyalty

and trust. In order to do great work for customers and deliver great results, employees also connect and collaborate with *vendors as partners*. They connect and collaborate in ways that benefit both sides *and* serve customers, rather than squeeze suppliers to improve margins. Business also needs thriving *communities* to flourish, and employees, who come from those communities and contribute to them, are central to that connection. The noble purpose also feeds the company's connection with communities. Finally, the connection between the company and its *shareholders* is fundamentally a human one. Shareholders are either individuals or companies who are themselves human organizations serving a human purpose. Asset management companies are looking after people's financial well-being and their retirements.

So, employees pursuing a noble purpose are the heart, and relationships are the blood that flows through the entire system and make it thrive. In this approach, all elements are connected in a closely interdependent, mutually reinforcing system.

Profits are an outcome of a successful strategy and the quality of the human relationships that drive it. But they are also essential to fulfill the mission, as they make it possible to invest in employees and innovation; create growth; support the community; and, of course, reward investors.

In summary, this approach is a declaration of interdependence.

I am excited about this approach and its underlying philosophy for several reasons.

First, it makes sense, both philosophically and spiritually. For me, it echoes the wisdom of some of the world's most important philosophers and religions, from Aristotle to Judeo-Christianism and Hinduism.

Second, it works. This is not just theory or wishful thinking. Over 25 years, I have seen close up how a purposeful, human organization creates great outcomes. I have seen it work at several companies—including Best Buy.

An Approach That Delivers

At its core, the resurgence of Best Buy is based on embracing and implementing these principles. It has propelled the company to heights that, back in 2012, few would have imagined possible. From the beginning of our turnaround, our approach was to look after *all* stakeholders, as is described in detail in chapter 7, and our noble purpose has been central to the way we have grown and evolved.

As you may have already guessed, Best Buy's purpose today is not about selling TVs or laptops. It is not about beating Walmart or Amazon.

Then what is it, and how did we land on it?

In 2015, once the turnaround of the company was completed, we spent time thinking about the way forward. We were no longer drowning, and with our head above water, we could spend energy figuring out where we wanted to swim.

During our quarterly senior leadership meeting, we reflected on how to articulate our noble purpose. There are many ways to frame a purpose, but what was Best Buy's? What defined the company and what it could be? We did left-brain analytical research, which highlighted that, although technology innovation was exciting, many customers needed help figuring out what it could do for them and how to take advantage of it. We also had to tap into right-brain creative and emotional dimensions. During one of these two-day offsites, we spent time over dinner sharing our life stories and personal purposes, which helped us gradually define what we collectively loved doing—one of the four dimensions of the purpose diagram presented in chapter 2. After two years or so, we eventually landed on a formulation for the company's purpose that felt right, a formulation that made business sense and just made sense, period. It had meaning for us as human beings.

Best Buy's purpose was *to enrich our customers' lives through technology*. We would do this by addressing their key human needs in areas such as entertainment, productivity, communication, food, security, and health and wellness.

Guided by this noble purpose and putting people first, Best Buy illustrates why this approach works: it opens new horizons; it is inspiring; and it ensures that economic activity is sustainable and produces great bottom-line results.

This approach expands horizons

A noble purpose creates an expansive and enduring vision that opens up new markets and opportunities. Enriching people's lives by addressing their key human needs through technology, for example, allows for many more activities than just selling consumer electronics. It expands what Best Buy can do.

This approach also allows a company to weather change. Twenty years from now, enriching the lives of customers through technology will still be relevant—even if TVs and personal computers no longer are. We will never be done enriching lives through technology, regardless of the technology. This purpose will keep stretching the company to be the best version of itself, rather than being better than someone else. Embracing this purpose has given Best Buy an ambitious, long-lasting, and aspirational goal. The company will never be done being the best it can be. Best Buy's purpose will never be fulfilled, and the journey will never end for as long as it keeps delivering for all its stakeholders.

This approach inspires people

Do you remember the two masons from chapter 2, and how one was cutting stones, and the other was building cathedrals? What is true for masons—and individuals in general—is also true for companies. A clear purpose is not just a strategic tool. To be effective, it must also inspire and guide. Cutting stones is tedious work. Building cathedrals is a noble purpose that inspires because it helps answer our human quest for meaning. Compare the dream of enriching lives through technology to the idea of selling TVs and computers. Or maximizing shareholder value. Which is more likely to pull you out of bed in the morning and fire you up? Whenever I remember my miserable summer sticking price tags on vegetable cans as a teenager, I think of Wegmans, the US chain of grocery stores whose mission is to help families live healthier, better lives through food. Besides its affordable quality products, Wegmans is famous for its happy employees. This is why articulating and integrating a noble purpose is a critical aspect of addressing the epidemic of worker disengagement.

Anthony Wu, a Blue Shirt from the Best Buy store in Mountain View, California, illustrates the difference between cutting stones and building cathedrals. A shopper tells Anthony she is looking for headphones, but she is not sure which ones to choose. Anthony has a choice. He can directly recommend the most sophisticated—and expensive— headphones. Or he can spend time understanding what she needs. He starts a conversation. Prompted by Anthony's interest, the woman explains that she works in a noisy open-space office, and she finds it hard to concentrate. She needs to block off some of the noise but wants to be able to communicate and hear when her colleagues need her. Anthony knows a lot about headphones, so once he understands her problem, he can recommend the ones that best solve that problem—which, it turns out, are not the most expensive. The customer is happy: she has found someone who listened and helped her. And Anthony feels good as well: he is not pushing headphones; he's made a positive difference in someone's daily life. This is authentic human connection at work.

This approach inspires more than employees. In his widely watched 2009 TED Talk, Simon Sinek argued that it is purpose—what he calls the "why"—that indeed sets the most inspiring leaders and organizations apart from others. The organizations that inspire deep loyalty from customers are those able to think, act, and communicate, starting from their purpose. "People don't buy what you do," says Simon Sinek; "people buy why you do it."[2]

This approach ensures that economic activity is sustainable

Let me be clear here: I deeply disagree with Milton Friedman's view that business has no business dealing with societal issues. There can be no thriving business without healthy, thriving communities, and there can be no thriving business if our planet is on fire. The Covid-19 pandemic has highlighted how healthy and thriving communities are essential for business health. Companies can decide how to play their part in addressing these issues, as is illustrated in chapter 6. But I believe they must play their part. Not only is this the right thing to do; it is also ultimately in their own interest.

This approach produces great bottom-line results

I love the joke about two engineers, one American and the other French. The French engineer presents his invention to his American colleague and explains the theory behind it. "Great," says the American engineer, "but does it work in practice?" Then the American operates his own invention. "Phenomenal," says the French engineer, "but does it work in theory?"

The purposeful human organization approach would satisfy both the American and the French engineers. It works in theory and in practice. In my experience, some of the most successful companies in the world have adopted these principles. Here are two that I know well, as I serve on their boards of directors.

The first is Ralph Lauren Corporation, a company that has defined its human purpose as *inspiring the dream of a better life through authenticity and timeless style.* "What I do," says Ralph Lauren himself, "is about living the best life you can and enjoying the fullness of the life around you—from what you wear to the way you live, to the way you love."[3] This means the company is not a clothes company, but a lifestyle business. That is far more inspiring for the people of Ralph Lauren—and farther reaching and longer lasting—than selling apparel. This is the cathedral they are building.

The second company is Johnson & Johnson. In the lobby of its headquarters in New Brunswick, New Jersey, stands an eight-foot-tall, six-ton slab of quartz and limestone. Carved in the stone is the company's Credo, four paragraphs first written in 1943, by the founder's son, just before the company became publicly traded. The Credo's fundamental principle is to put the needs and well-being of the people the company serves first. It defines Johnson & Johnson's responsibilities to its customers, employees, and stockholders, as well as local and world communities.[4] It has been revised several times, but its basic principles have not changed. The company sees its Credo not only as its moral compass but also as its guiding light in making decisions and the recipe for its enduring business success.

When companies embrace this approach to business, as Best Buy, Ralph Lauren, and Johnson & Johnson have, they can become "firms of endearment"—a term coined by Raj Sisodia, Jag Sheth, and David Wolfe.[5] These firms—among them Whole Foods, 3M, and Timberland—have built high-performance businesses producing superior financial results based on purpose, self-actualization, and genuine partnerships that benefit all stakeholders. They are at the forefront of transforming capitalism. They have outperformed the S&P 500 by 14 times over a period of 15 years.[6] This confirms that a business can do good by making a positive difference in people's lives *and* be extremely successful for its shareholders, because that success is built on the fact that it conducts business responsibly.

Multiple other studies have confirmed that purpose indeed pays.[7] Companies that Barron's magazine ranks as America's most sustainable (including Best Buy) generated average financial returns of over 34 percent for their stockholders in 2019, above the S&P 500 Index's 31.5 percent. Their purposeful and human approach guides good strategies, and it attracts and keeps talented employees who are engaged. Their strong environmental policies lower costs, and customers increasingly want to spend their money on brands that, besides serving their needs well, have adopted good sustainable practices.[8]

A Revolution in the Making

The idea that the purpose of business is to contribute to the common good and that it must look after all stakeholders—hence the "stakeholder capitalism" catchphrase—has made significant headway in the past decade.

An increasing number of business leaders are embracing this approach. In 2018, I received BlackRock leader Larry Fink's annual letter to CEOs of companies in which the asset management company holds shares. "To prosper over time, every company must not only deliver financial performance, but also show how it makes a positive contribution to society," Fink wrote. "Without a sense of purpose, no company, either public or private, can achieve its full potential."[9] BlackRock has been actively nudging the companies in which it holds shares to define and articulate their broader purpose—one that makes a positive contribution to society—and to clearly manifest that purpose in the company's business model and strategy.

I was excited about Larry's letter. This was so aligned with my own beliefs. I was also thrilled that Larry used his voice and considerable influence to push for change. This convincingly contradicted the notion that shareholders care only about share price and quarterly results. Coming from the largest asset management firm in the world, the call to focus on a broader purpose instead of short-term profit, on all stakeholders instead of only shareholders, and on a long-term horizon instead of market myopia carries real weight.

In my own letter to Best Buy's shareholders that year, I responded to Larry Fink's challenge. I laid out Best Buy's noble purpose, which had formally been introduced at our investor meeting a few months earlier. I explained how the idea of enriching lives through technology anchored not only our Building the New Blue growth strategy but also the way the company related to employees, customers, vendors, the environment, and our local communities. Because BlackRock is one of Best Buy's shareholders, I decided to hand-deliver my letter to Larry Fink, which I did that July at BlackRock's headquarters in midtown Manhattan. This gave me the opportunity to thank Larry for his leadership.

Then, in August 2019, the Business Roundtable, whose members are the CEOs of the United States' leading companies,[10] issued a new statement on the purpose of corporations. "Each of our stakeholders is essential," it read. "We commit to deliver value to *all* of them, for the future success of our companies, our communities and our country."[11] This was quite a shift from the organization's 1997 position that corporations exist primarily to serve shareholders. The 181 CEOs who signed the Business Roundtable statement in August 2019 undertook to deliver value to their customers, invest in their employees, deal fairly and ethically with their suppliers, support the communities in which their companies work, *and*—yes—generate long-term value for their shareholders as well, of course. "While each of our individual companies serves its own corporate purpose, we share a fundamental commitment to *all* of our stakeholders," the statement said.[12]

I am heartened to see this vision advancing elsewhere. In May 2019, for example, France enacted a new law that revised the civil code's definition of corporate purpose—for the first time since 1804—as the common interest of stockholders. The change follows recommendations from CEOs. Corporations must now consider the social and environmental impact of their activities. Corporations are also now able to explicitly define a raison d'être—a purpose beyond profits—in their charter.

This is a revolution, and business has unprecedented power, resources, and reach to carry it forward. Based on 2017 revenues, 69 out of the richest 100 entities in the world are corporations, not governments.[13] Given the power and the global reach business enjoys, it can—and must—be part of the solution and help address the challenges that my children and I were discussing at that Christmas dinner. When the United States withdrew from the Paris Accord, for example, a number of companies responded by committing to meeting the agreement's emission targets even faster, something that makes sense for the planet and for business as well. This kind of activism must continue to grow. If it does, it will transform business and capitalism from the inside out.

But skepticism remains. Many do not believe business leaders and shareholders are sincere in their shift toward purpose and stakeholder capitalism. They see this as lip service to placate customers and employees.

The gap that lies between today's reality and my vision is not between words and intention, however. It is between intention and practice. The business leaders I know are genuinely convinced that the system has to change[14]—and they know that employees, customers, and investors will eventually clobber anyone who is pretending and content with window dressing.

But good intentions alone or shortcuts will not result in the required change. All they will produce are hollow visions and mission statements that exist only on companies' websites. Creating a purposeful human organization that truly unleashes human magic and makes a positive difference in the world is not only complex, but it is also hard work. It influences every aspect of the business—both in good times and in challenging ones. It requires a fundamental rethinking of management and leadership.

It's not easy, but it is necessary. How can companies make such profound change happen? This is what is explored in the next few chapters.

Questions to Reflect On

- Has the company you work at done a good job of articulating an inspiring noble purpose?

- Has it translated that purpose into developing meaningful relationships with its customers, its employees, its vendors, its shareholders, and the communities in which it operates?

- Is the whole thing working?

- If not, what would it take to get there?

6

Putting a Noble Purpose to Work

The Devil is in the details, but so is salvation.

—Admiral Hyman G. Rickover, US Navy

Stanley is a senior recuperating at home after a double lung transplant. He receives a call from a Best Buy care agent, who asks Stanley how he is doing. Very well, Stanley tells the agent.

But Stanley was not doing very well, and the care agent knew it. Thanks to a number of sensors placed in Stanley's home and artificial intelligence analyzing the data they send, the agent could surmise whether Stanley was eating and sleeping properly, and whether he was moving around enough or using the bathroom. The agent saw that Stanley was not opening his fridge nearly often enough for someone eating regularly. Trained to engage with seniors like Stanley, the agent was able to confirm that, despite his assurances that he was fine, Stanley was not eating enough. In fact, he was struggling to keep his food down. The agent then organized help for Stanley.

It is one thing to talk about noble purpose and putting people at the center of an organization, but what does that look like in practice? When I am asked this, I tell stories like this one. Helping aging customers live at home safely is enriching lives through technology. Still, how do you ensure that purpose is deeply rooted within the company such that it guides every aspect of business and shows up in operations in real ways, like it did with Stanley?

This is not easy. It requires making the noble purpose the keystone of the corporate strategy, embracing and mobilizing all stakeholders, and aligning management practices. These efforts typically require a fundamental rethink of how we do business, moving past practices that many leaders, including myself, were trained to embrace as immutable truths.

Making a Noble Purpose the Keystone of the Company's Strategy

Best Buy's noble purpose of enriching lives through technology did not just stay on some presentation slide. It fundamentally changed our strategy and how we did business. It unleashed significant innovation and growth. After several months of intense data analysis, we identified entertainment, productivity, communications, food, security, and health and wellness as the key human needs we wanted to address. This is where we could enrich lives through technology. And we would do it by moving from a business focused on transactions and selling products to one that developed solutions and lasting customer relationships.

The service Stanley used was one manifestation of this decision.

Serving seniors with health-care services passed our four-question test: it fit the company purpose; it was good for customers; we could deliver; and Best Buy could make money. Ten thousand people turn 65 years old every day in the United States, and people are living longer. Most seniors want to stay home as long as possible as they age, even though two-thirds live with at least one chronic condition. The home health service enriches their lives, but also the lives of their children and caregivers. It provides an alternative to increasingly expensive assisted living. It also benefits the health-care and insurance industries, helping keep costs down.

If we had not linked our purpose to our strategy, we would not have recognized opportunities now bearing fruit for Best Buy, like offering "total tech support" and deploying in-home advisors. The point is to enrich lives through technology, so Best Buy's Geek Squad helps you with your tech regardless of where you bought it. And in-home advisors make house calls to provide tech solutions that are best designed on-site, not in the store. Best Buy's advisors become like your personal "chief technology officer" over time. This helps customers, who can develop a lasting relationship with a pro, who is able to help them make the most of technology. And it helps Best Buy, as finding new ways to help customers brings in new revenues and profit.

People were convinced that Best Buy was going to die in 2012 because consumer electronics was not growing much and was increasingly commoditized. Maybe Best Buy would have died if our strategy reflected the idea that we were a store that sold consumer electronics. But building a strategy from the more expansive lens of our noble purpose changed the game. Our environment was actually rich with opportunities. The web of initiatives that was our "Best Buy 2020: Building the New Blue" growth strategy, launched in 2017 once the company's turnaround was complete, all linked back to that one purpose: the dream of enriching customers' lives through technology.

Approaching strategy this way, though, goes against the grain of some established practices. Traditionally, strategy is articulated around being the best or first in a category, the way GE always strove to be number one or two in its market segments. I have done this too. When I was CEO of Carlson Wagonlit Travel, I wanted us to overtake

American Express's corporate travel business for the number-one spot. But winning a race against another company cannot and should not dictate strategy. Such ambitions create zero-sum games that narrow strategy and execution. Also, they are not particularly inspiring, meaningful, or fulfilling.

Imagine you are responsible for the strategy of a health and life insurance company. If your purpose is defined in terms of profits, then your best strategy is about making sure your customers use your services as little as possible. Your customer interaction will focus on collecting premiums and managing claims. If, however, you define your noble purpose as helping people live healthier lives, then the strategy changes, radically.

This is how Discovery, a global financial services company from South Africa, has defined its purpose. Because of that, its strategy has produced Vitality, a business model that turns traditional insurance on its head. Using behavioral economics and clinical science, the company partners with tech companies, grocery and retail stores, gyms, and more to offer a wide range of incentives, games, and events that nudge Vitality members to exercise, eat well, and get their health checked regularly. The business model also allows for a dynamic pricing of risk. The result? Frequent, rewarding interactions with customers keep them loyal. Healthier behavior improves their lives, as well as local communities, by reducing health-care burden and costs. Resulting profits benefit the company, its vendors, and shareholders. Everyone benefits from this "shared-value insurance."

Embracing and Mobilizing All Stakeholders

When French CEO Jean-Marie Descarpentries held court at that McKinsey dinner all those years ago, he told me that, in his view, 98 percent of questions asked as either/or are better answered with "and."

That was another break from what I was used to at the time, a world of binary decisions: Should we focus on cost *or* revenues? Cost *or* quality? Should we take care of our customers *or* our employees *or* our shareholders? Should we partner with our vendors *or* compete? Should we worry about the environment and the community *or* focus on profits? Should we focus on the long term *or* short term?

I now believe, as Jean-Marie did, that these either/or questions are artificial trade-offs. We maximize performance not by choosing between stakeholders, but by embracing and mobilizing all of them. We choose employees *and* customers *and* shareholders *and* the community.

If, like me, you were trained to put profits first, you might dismiss this as overly optimistic. I will not say it is easy, but reframing zero-sum games can be done. Here are some ways Best Buy did it.

Delighting customers

After we formulated Best Buy's noble purpose, it quickly became apparent that we had a lot more work to do. Something was missing: most employees did not grasp what it concretely meant for them and their work. Unless they could, the company's noble purpose would fail to become reality.

"We have to start from within," Mike Mohan told me. It was 2017, and Mike, who later became the company's president and COO, was working with then–chief marketing officer Whit Alexander on the reinvention of the company. At Best Buy, they said, enriching lives through technology had to start with people—our people.

What do we look like when we are at our best? If Best Buy were a person, how would she or he behave? To answer that question, we ran a series of workshops involving leaders who knew the company best. From those workshops, we settled on the idea that the company, through its sales associates, was an "inspiring friend" who helps customers understand what they want to do and imagine how technology can help them.

From this, we defined how that "inspiring friend"—whom everyone at the company was expected to embody—would behave to deliver on that promise. "Be human" was one expected behavior. To clarify what this meant in practice, we rolled out workshops across all US stores. On a Saturday morning, staff in each store met at 7:30 a.m. for two hours. Did they watch some video from the chief marketing officer or the CEO? No. The store general manager first walked them through the basic idea behind the expected behaviors. Then he or she launched a discussion during which sales associates shared their own stories with each other and explained how a friend had particularly inspired them.

I attended this training in a New York City store. One associate explained how she ended up homeless after escaping an abusive boyfriend and how Best Buy was her family. I shared how I have always admired my older brother Phillippe for his boundless energy and kind generosity.

Once they had experienced how to "be human" among themselves, it became clear how everyone could relate to customers in the same way—when helping seniors like Stanley or customers looking for the right headphones. Everyone at the company participated in these workshops, including the board of directors.

It wasn't the first time I had experienced how putting people and customers ahead of an obsessive focus on short-term profits pays off. Shortly after I became CEO of the video game division of Vivendi in 1999, I went to Irvine to meet the team that ran Blizzard Entertainment. If you are into video games, I do not need to introduce Blizzard. Its blockbuster titles such as *Diablo* and the *World of Warcraft* turned it into the Pixar of video games. As soon as I stepped into the office, I was struck by everyone's singular focus to create the most epic games possible. It practically oozed from the walls. All employees, from the receptionist to the president, were avid gamers. They not only had a direct connection to their customers—they *were* the customers. They involved dedicated gamers in development, integrating their feedback. They were religious about quality and wanted their games to be as fun as possible for as many people as possible.

I sat with cofounder and president Mike Morhaime. "Let's agree now that you are not going to decide when the games are released," he told me. There would be no pressure to push new games out before they were absolutely ready. Being late did not matter, as long as games were great. The team understood that financial results were an outcome. They understood that the core of the company's success was the relationship with its customers, the cult-like following of millions of subscribers around the world—*World of Warcraft* alone had 12 million monthly subscribers in 2010. Compromising on quality or timing by publishing games before they were the best possible would have dented that following—and only hurt financial results over the long term. I could see how this approach was great not only for Blizzard's customers but for our shareholders as well.

Partnering with vendors and competitors

Arm wrestling with suppliers to minimize costs and improve margins is a good thing, especially in a turnaround, right? Yes, dealing with suppliers involves some arm wrestling. But this does not exclude partnering in a way that benefits both sides. The way Best Buy has worked with its vendors, including those who are supposed to be its competitors, has been a key ingredient of its resurgence and illustrates how such partnerships transcend a view of the business world as a zero-sum game.

When I joined Best Buy, we were in a strange position with many of our vendors, from Apple and Microsoft to Sony. They were developing their own retail stores, which could compete with ours. At the same time, Best Buy operated thousands of stores that offered the kind of proximity and reach they needed to commercialize their technology. I knew from my experience in the travel industry that vendors could be a source of revenue for us. And we needed a way to cover our costs: shortly after I started, we had decided to match online prices to discourage "showrooming"—when potential customers come to the store for advice and to try products out but end up buying online. Best Buy needed its suppliers, and suppliers needed Best Buy. There had to be ways we could help each other, possibly through strategic partnerships.

During my first week on the job at Best Buy, I said as much to the Minneapolis *Star Tribune*. J. K. Shin, then co–chief executive of Samsung Electronics, took me at my word and flew to Minneapolis to discuss the idea. Over dinner, we explored how we could create Samsung mini-stores exclusively within Best Buy stores. This store-within-a-store idea would save Samsung much time and capital while also giving customers keen to try out Samsung's hot new Galaxy products good reasons to visit Best Buy stores. Samsung could focus on product and innovation while Best Buy would take care of retail. This made so much sense for both companies and for our customers. By the end of dinner, we shook hands on it.

We unveiled the Samsung Experience—the brand's showcase—at the Best Buy store in New York City's Union Square a few months later. It worked. Soon, there were Samsung Experience mini-stores in all Best Buy stores around the country, helping Samsung ramp up its sales in the United States and helping us offset our costs.

We applied the same model with other suppliers, including Microsoft, Sony, LG, AT&T, Verizon, Sprint, Canon, Nikon, and Google. The strategy contributed to revitalizing Sony's ailing TV business. Apple, with whom we had developed the first store-within-a-store experience back in 2007, also decided to double down and invest more in our space, even though they had their own flagship retail fleet. And in 2019, Apple announced that Best Buy would service Apple products, helping the many customers who do not live near an Apple store. Great for the customers, great for Apple, and great for Best Buy, as this meant another reason for customers to visit our stores.

If Best Buy had remained a company whose mission was to sell electronics, showrooming might well have killed us, as more and more customers used us to look at products and then ordered them from Amazon. But we found ways to effectively partner with the world's foremost tech companies around our redefined purpose so that, now, they finance their own brand corners in our stores, including marketing and staff training. We transformed *showrooming* into what we call *showcasing.*

And so, if you walk into a Best Buy store today, you will find an Apple store, a Microsoft store, and a Samsung store, as well as Sony, LG, and Google stores.

And an Amazon store.

Yes, Amazon, the disruptive competitor, the Goliath that was supposed to kill us.

We had always sold Amazon's products—beginning with the Kindle tablet. As Amazon expanded their product line to include a vast array of Alexa-enabled products, we dedicated space to them and did live demos right next to the equivalent space dedicated to Google's competing products. Whereas the world saw Amazon as an existential threat to Best Buy, we saw another mutually beneficial partnership that could become a showcasing success story.

An even bigger opportunity came in 2018 around Amazon's new FireTV platform. At a press conference in our Bellevue store across the water from Amazon's Seattle headquarters, Jeff Bezos and I jointly announced an expanded partnership. Amazon gave Best Buy the exclusive rights to sell FireTV embedded in smart TVs. The only place to buy nearly a dozen models would be at a Best Buy store and through Best Buy on Amazon.com.

"A TV is a considered purchase," Jeff explained during the press conference. "People do want to come in and see the TV. They want to experiment with the TV—try it out."

The *Star Tribune* found the moment surreal. "Jeff Bezos, whose company many once thought would put Best Buy out of business, not only trading compliments with his competitor, but also acknowledging he could use its help to sell products," it read.[1]

"Physical stores aren't going anywhere," Jeff said. "E-commerce is going to be a part of everything, but not the whole thing."[2]

This "coup" was in fact the natural extension of putting purpose and people at the heart of business. Jeff told me that the trust that our two teams had built working together over the previous years had been essential to his decision to partner so closely.

Helping the community thrive

As you know from chapter 5, I strongly believe that it is business's business to get involved in societal issues.

But how can a company decide what causes to prioritize and pursue? When is it right to take a stand and act—and when not? How do you avoid the trap that many corporate social responsibility (CSR) programs seem to fall into, turning into haphazard collections of unrelated initiatives that suffer from poor coordination, often without active involvement from the CEO?[3]

By aligning the company's agenda with its noble purpose and by ensuring it is part of its strategy instead of a random afterthought. Take the environment: the future of business depends heavily on the future of our planet. Not surprisingly, a growing number of companies are incorporating fighting climate change and environmental degradation into how they do business.

I am proud of the fact that Best Buy reduced its carbon footprint by 55 percent over the last 10 years, for example by rolling out LED lights throughout our stores and using hybrid cars for Geek Squad agents. This helps the environment and helped us save money on our energy consumption. Again, not a zero-sum game.

Making a significant difference will increasingly involve cooperating with other industry players. Collective action creates greater impact faster. If a critical mass within an industry joins forces toward a collective pledge, then competitive considerations cannot be used as an excuse for inaction. One example is the initiative announced in August 2019 at the G7 summit in Biarritz by fashion's biggest and most influential companies, including French luxury giant Kering, Adidas, Chanel, Nike, and Ralph Lauren. Their pact addresses the industry's impact on climate change, biodiversity, and ocean pollution. The brands involved in the pact make up over 30 percent of fashion's production volume. This is the kind of collective action—among companies but also between business and NGOs, governments, and aid agencies—that Paul Polman, the former CEO of Unilever, is going after with Imagine, the corporation and foundation he cofounded and chairs. Imagine, which was instrumental in bringing together CEOs to commit to the Fashion Pact, is looking at how to build scale—fast. Critics point out that the pact is not perfect. But such collective and concerted action is a step in the right direction.[4]

Addressing the severe inequalities that exist in the communities in which we operate is another priority. For its part, Best Buy has been building and deploying Best Buy Teen Tech Centers to offer hands-on technology training to kids from underserved communities that prepares them for potential career paths. As of the end of 2020, there were nearly 40 of these centers. Best Buy vendors helped build them, highlighting that business can use its collective strengths to do good. Companies can support local communities in a multitude of ways. But initiatives are far more powerful, far reaching, and successful when they align with the company's purpose, as they become an extension of the business, instead of an arbitrary add-on.

Many businesses have also mobilized around social issues that their current and future workforce deeply care about, such as education, immigration, and the rights of minorities. Founder and co-CEO of Salesforce Marc Benioff's decisive action in support of LGBTQ+ rights, even if it risked affecting the bottom line, was a watershed moment. Benioff called it a fork in the road for the company and for his role as its CEO. His public stand gave Salesforce even more visibility, and the company continued to post record earnings. It also sent a clear signal to employees about the company's values. "Gone are the days when companies can recruit and retain top talent without upholding a commitment to values," he concludes. "No business will succeed in the future until it embraces the notion that values *create* value."[5]

One of Best Buy's public stands started one early morning at the end of August 2017. I was in my office, catching up on the news, when I came across a letter signed by a number of business leaders from the West Coast, addressed to President Trump and all leaders of Congress. The Trump administration had announced that it would repeal the Deferred Action for Childhood Arrivals (DACA) program, which allowed Dreamers—immigrants who had arrived illegally in the United States as young children—to study and work legally in the United States. The open letter was urging political leaders to maintain the protection granted to Dreamers and pass legislation toward a permanent solution.

As in many major US companies, some of our employees were Dreamers, and the political arm wrestling in Washington made them enormously anxious. We had to protect them. As an immigrant myself, the situation struck a deep chord in me. But more broadly, nearly 800,000 young people who had registered in good faith into the program, 97 percent of whom were working or in school, were suddenly facing immediate deportation. This transcended the debate over immigration. It was about fairness and humanity. Why wasn't Best Buy part of this collective action?

We had to do something, and we had to do something urgently. I called Matt Furman, who was in charge of communications and public affairs. By the end of the day, I had signed the open letter, adding my voice and our company's to the chorus of business leaders who had taken a stand. I also assured our employees that Best Buy stood by them and would provide legal help if they needed it.

A month later, Best Buy cofounded the Coalition for the American Dream, dedicated to finding a permanent solution for Dreamers. Unfortunately, that solution has so far remained elusive, and the battle continues through the courts. In October 2019, we joined an amicus brief filed with the US Supreme Court to support the DACA program. On June 18, 2020, the Supreme Court rejected the Trump administration's attempt to end the Deferred Action for Childhood Arrivals program. This provides a reprieve, which will hopefully give enough time to find a permanent solution for Dreamers. In the meantime, we will continue to take a stand for what we feel is right.

Rewarding shareholders

Looking after *all* stakeholders in no way means marginalizing shareholders. Let me be clear: the problem is not shareholders, but considering shareholders as a faceless, heartless monolith that has to be favored at the expense of all other stakeholders. I have found that when you treat shareholders as human beings, they are not the short-term, profit-obsessed monsters they are sometimes portrayed to be. Best Buy has explicitly communicated to its shareholders that the company's purpose is not to make money. We did in November 2012 when we unveiled the Renew Blue turnaround plan: even when we were looking business death in the face, the plan covered all of our stakeholders. I did it again in April 2019 at an investor conference, and I felt then that they completely understood this approach to business.

It is easier than you may think to get shareholders on board, because having a noble purpose and looking after all stakeholders tends to result in great outcomes for shareholders. Best Buy stock price went from a low of $11 in November 2012 to more than $110 as I write these lines some eight years later.

Putting human relationships at the heart of business means treating everyone well—including investors and analysts who do not like our stock. For several years, one of the financial analysts following Best Buy maintained his "sell" recommendation throughout our turnaround and recovery. We could have gotten frustrated. Why couldn't he see the progress we were making? But he was doing his job, advising his own customers to the best of his ability. So, our investor relations team treated him with as much care as any other analyst. Eventually, even he threw in the towel and changed his recommendation. So, treat everyone as a customer, as a human being with real needs. Quite the revolution!

. . .

Once we reject the view of the business world as a zero-sum game, there is no limit to the power of "and." Business can do well by doing good. Best Buy is addressing the needs of aging Americans like Stanley *and* growing an entirely new business. Our electronics recycling program saves valuable metals *and* drives traffic to the stores by providing a real service to customers. Investing in energy-efficient LED lights helps reduce carbon emission *and* reduces our operational costs by saving energy. Investing in the Best Buy Teen Tech Centers supports underserved communities by helping disadvantaged teenagers acquire skills *and* helps Best Buy diversify its workforce.

I believe that the key to business success and addressing our world's most burning challenges—those that bother my children and so many in their generation—entails embracing and mobilizing customers *and* vendors *and* communities *and* shareholders in pursuit of a chosen noble purpose. Doing so happens when a company's employees connect with all of them with heart.

Aligning Management Practices

Moving to a model that focuses on purpose and people requires changing key management practices. At Best Buy, this reflected Jean-Marie Descarpentries's People → Business → Finance approach.

In practice, this means resetting how you spend your time and interact with others. For example, when I was CEO at Best Buy, I adopted the practice of starting monthly business reviews by first discussing employees, then customers, before getting into financials. This is unusual, but it is a tangible way to reflect that sequence. I always presented my updates to Best Buy's board of directors following that same sequence. Even during the turnaround of Best Buy, when the company's survival was at stake, we spent more time focusing on people and how we could fix the business, and less on financials.

It took me some time to learn this. When I was president of EDS France, I spent hours dissecting financial reports and asking endless questions about the numbers, getting involved in minute details. I enjoy numbers and analysis; this was satisfying. And in spite of adopting the People → Business → Finance approach, I still slipped back into old habits when results were disappointing. But I now realize that it achieved nothing beyond driving my team crazy. Letting the company's CFO do his or her job was a skill and a discipline I had to acquire.

Best Buy's Holiday Leadership Meeting, which brings together store managers from all over the country to kick off the holiday season, provides another illustration of how management practices must and can evolve. Clearly, the holiday season at Best Buy is critical to the company's success. Our fourth quarter alone accounts for half of the year's profit. So, you would think everything in the holiday leadership meeting would be focused on how we are going to maximize the outcome. Not so. The last meeting I attended, in the fall of 2019, started with front liners' and managers' personal stories about what inspires them.

The stage was at the center of the room, not at the front. The CEO did not speak until day two. In the same vein, this annual gathering always kicks off with charitable activities, such as building computers for disadvantaged kids, to remind everyone that humanity—not financial results—is at the heart of the business.

We also changed management practices by changing metrics. Key performance indicators (KPIs) ought to go beyond financials or rankings. Instruments to measure progress with all stakeholders have multiplied over the years, from employee surveys and net promoter scores measuring customer experience, to carbon footprints, to diversity achievements. Accounting standards are being developed to incorporate considerations like environmental impact. Tools to measure how well purpose is embedded in a company's practices are beginning to emerge.[6]

These measures are not perfect. But no measure is, so imperfection is no excuse for inaction. Those who hide behind the notion that they cannot do this because the metrics are not ideal remind me of the story of the man who loses his keys on the street at night. He desperately searches for them in the glow of a streetlight. "Are you sure you have lost your keys here?" asks his friend. "No," he replies, "but this is the only area where there is light."

We can go further and we should, especially with external metrics that can impel internal change. Rating agencies, financial analysts, and proxy advisors—companies that advise shareholders to inform their votes at shareholders meetings—are increasingly considering a broader range of measures when assessing companies' performance and prospects, though there is still some lag. Proxy advisors, for example, still tend to look only at shareholder returns when assessing executive compensation.

The journey to develop and adopt better, more balanced, more broadly accepted measures of performance needs to continue.

. . .

All of this noble purpose and connecting with heart business sounds great, you might think—until you hit a tough patch. Then reality takes over, and you have to resort to good old recipes, right?

The story of Best Buy's turnaround demonstrates that this approach is not limited to companies that do well. In fact, as shown in chapter 7, it has been the main reason behind the company's revival.

Questions to Reflect On

- How does your company's strategy reflect its noble purpose?

- Does the way your company relates to its employees, customers, vendors, local communities, and shareholders fully align with its purpose?

- Do you tend to adopt an "either/or" approach, or are you able to address challenges through "and"? Can you reframe a current problem to unlock a win–win solution?

- What do you discuss first during meetings? People, business, or finance?

- How does your company measure how well it is doing with employees, customers, suppliers, communities, and shareholders?

7

How to Turn around a Business without Everyone Hating You

It was the best of times, it was the worst of times.

—Charles Dickens, *A Tale of Two Cities*

Here is a typical scenario: company struggles; company announces job cuts, layoffs, restructuring; Wall Street applauds; share price goes up as thousands of employees go out the door. We have seen this movie before and heard its soundtrack of fear, anger, and disbelief. Plus, this movie often has sequels, with multiple rounds of restructuring. Turnarounds have come to be viewed as a kind of blood sport, a race to the bottom, a vicious slashing of headcount, spending, and customer service.

How can this make any sense?

In my view, putting purpose and people at the heart of business, and the practical implications of that model outlined in the previous chapters, are not luxuries reserved for thriving businesses. In fact, this approach forms the very core of the "turnaround manual" I have developed over the years, based on what I have learned from my own experience at Best Buy and elsewhere, as well as from studying other corporate rescues. By the time I decided to follow Jim Citrin's advice and go for the Best Buy job, I had led or been involved in half-a-dozen turnarounds. That experience gave me the confidence to embark on what turned out to be an amazing adventure, when so many of my friends in Minneapolis thought I was crazy.

The principles in this "manual" are the antithesis of the blood sport I described above. It is the opposite of "cut, cut, cut." When a business is in critical condition, its people are the key to a successful turnaround. Survival depends on them, how energized they are, and how much they care about customers and all other stakeholders. I am not advocating for a soft, sitting-around-the-campfire roasting-s'mores focus on people. I mean a mobilizing, energizing, making-things-happen-fast focus on people.

The story of Renew Blue, Best Buy's turnaround plan launched in the fall of 2012, illustrates how to unleash the human energy and connections that are particularly relevant, meaningful, and effective during crises and hard times. But instead of following the chronology of events, I will tell the story through the underlying principles that guided our turnaround: always start with people; always end with people; and generate human energy.

Starting with People—Always

September 4, 2012, was the first day of my new job as CEO of Best Buy. But instead of driving to the company's headquarters in Richfield, Minnesota, I drove about 60 miles north of Minneapolis, to St. Cloud, a town hugging the Mississippi River at the heart of the state's farmland. I would spend my first three days on the job working in the town's Best Buy store on Division Street.

Learning from front liners

I was new not only to Best Buy but to retail in general, and I had a lot to learn. I also knew that listening to front liners was the best way to do that. Wearing my khaki pants and the iconic Best Buy Blue Shirt with a "CEO in Training" tag, I spent my first day meeting the staff, listening, asking questions, walking up and down the store, visiting every department, observing sales associates interact with customers, and asking more questions. After my shift, I had dinner with the store management team at a local pizzeria. We spent the evening chatting and getting to know each other while also discussing what was working well for them and what was not. These were people coming face to face with customers every day, having to do their job with whatever tools had been given to them.

They knew a lot about what was really going on at Best Buy. A lot! During that dinner, for example, one of the sales associates pointed out that the bestbuy.com website's search engine was a problem. Customers could not find what they were looking for. She demonstrated by typing "Cinderella" in the search bar. The search engine spat out a list of Nikon cameras. I could not believe it.

Over dessert, I also found out that the employees were unhappy that employee discounts had been reduced several months earlier. Part of the reason many Blue Shirts worked at Best Buy was because they loved electronics, and the decision to push back a perk that they dearly valued bit hard. Even more galling, they said, was the board's decision at about the same time to introduce "stay bonuses" for certain senior executives to entice them to keep their jobs as the company was going through turmoil.

The next day, I had lunch with Matt Noska, the store's general manager. Just as with my mystery shopper experience, I had noticed earlier in the day that CDs, DVDs, and video games took up a lot of floor space. I grabbed a napkin and asked Matt if he would draw a rough picture of the store's floor plan. His sketch showed that about a fifth of the floor space was dedicated to physical media, which was fast losing ground to online streaming. Mobile phones, on the other hand, occupied only a tiny piece of the store space (4 percent), even though demand for them was booming. Small appliances such as juicers, blenders, and coffee machines were also popular and profitable—a market worth some $16 billion in the United States, and growing.[1] Unfortunately, they were virtually invisible in St. Cloud. I found one lonely blender on a shelf hidden at the back of the store. All this was clearly a great opportunity.

Back in the store, I observed customers. I saw that they would talk to Blue Shirts for a while and sometimes leave without buying anything. They were showrooming—getting advice and sampling products but buying online where, they thought, they would get cheaper prices. This left sales associates dispirited.

I was curious to understand why, in the Blue Shirts' opinions, customers should turn to Best Buy. What did we offer that other retailers did not? Associates had developed their own views as best they could, but they were neither consistent nor particularly compelling. This made me realize that the company had not given the Blue Shirts clear answers to this critical question—which meant that customers could not possibly know why they should turn to Best Buy either.

During a meeting in his office near the end of my time there, Matt Noska told me that Best Buy headquarters had piled on 30 or 40 indicators to measure the store's performance, from store card applications and extended warranties to how many accessories were being sold by product category. Every central department was pushing its own metrics and saying theirs were top priority, making it impossible for front liners and managers to know what they should focus on. Never mind that these metrics were not particularly useful or centered on customers. Store staff were disconcerted, confused, and overwhelmed. I could see how it was hurting the brand in the eyes of customers.

What I learned in these first few days, listening to store employees and observing what was going on in the store, I could never have fathomed poring over spreadsheets or sitting in meeting rooms with other executives in HQ. After a few days listening to my new colleagues and observing their work, I had gotten so many ideas about what we could do—and do quickly—to start fixing the business. When a business is in trouble, listening to the individuals on the front line is the best place to quickly identify what "crazy, goofy, or stupid" things, as I later told store managers, have been getting in the way. Best Buy's turnaround started with Blue Shirts in St. Cloud.

Choosing the right people at the top

Starting with people also means making sure you have the right executive team. If a business is doing well, credit goes to front liners. If it is struggling, top management has to be held accountable; like Mao Zedong, I believe that fish rots from the head.

Best Buy was struggling, so top management should be held accountable. But that did not mean I just started swapping out team members. I told the executive team on day one that everyone started with an "A." It was up to them to maintain their "A."

Sometimes the process is self-selecting. It did not take long to recognize which members of the executive team were not capable or willing to deliver what was needed and had to go.

We promoted a few leaders from within, including executives who successfully grew our mobile business. We also brought in new people. I was lucky to convince Sharon McCollam, who had been CFO and

COO of Williams-Sonoma, the successful multichannel retailer, to come out of retirement and join us as CFO. She was the woman we needed: investors respected her; she had fantastic experience in e-commerce; and she was a very hands-on, operational finance chief. Additionally, Scott Durchslag brought his expertise and experience from Expedia to run Best Buy's e-commerce.

Changes in management also energized people lower in the organization who recognized these changes as a strong signal that we were serious about performance.

Starting with people also meant mending fences with Dick Schulze, who had founded Best Buy and was still the company's largest shareholder.

Building one team with one dream

In May 2012, Dick Schulze had stepped down as Best Buy's chairman of the board—before I was approached to become the company's new CEO. By the time I started in September, he had launched an offensive to take the company private and was at war with the board. A company fighting with its founder seemed crazy to me. I greatly admired what Dick had accomplished and said so to our employees. Whether we were going to be private or public, he would remain Best Buy's founder and largest shareholder, and I wanted to build a positive relationship with him. I knew Brad Anderson, who had been Dick's right-hand man for years and Best Buy's CEO between 2002 and 2009. I asked him to introduce me to Dick, and he did.

In October, a month after my stint in St. Cloud, I headed to Dick Schulze's family foundation office, a few minutes from Best Buy's headquarters. I entered Dick's office, wearing a suit and tie, and handed him my résumé. "Under normal circumstances, you would have interviewed me," I explained. "So I wanted to introduce myself properly." Dick later told me that my gesture had touched him.

Dick and I could not have been more different: he had spent his entire life building a retail business, and I had no retail experience. He knew Best Buy inside out, and I was an outsider. Still, we managed to find common ground. Dick immediately struck me as a genuinely good, caring human being. He was simply worried about the trajectory of the business he had built and wanted to do something about it. I shared with him some of my basic business philosophies about people and customers. I also shared that I had no intention of blindly slashing stores or headcount, both of which I considered Best Buy's great strengths. By the end of our conversation, the ice had been broken.

The next month, at Thanksgiving, I flew to Dick's home in Florida with Hatim Tyabji, the chairman of Best Buy's board at the time. By then, we had told investors how we proposed to turn around Best Buy. Hatim and I wanted to explore how we could work with Dick and Brad to help restore Best Buy's health. It was clear that we all were eager to act in the company's best interest. Hatim, for example, indicated that he would have no problem stepping down as chairman of the board, if that was an issue. But it was also clear we were not yet totally aligned. During discussions at his lawyer's office, Dick generously offered to keep me as CEO should his attempt to buy out the company succeed. He then added that my mission would be to execute the plan he had developed together with Brad and Al Lenzmeier, the company's former CFO and COO. "I am really very good at taking input," I respectfully told him, "but I am terrible at taking directions. As, I suspect, you are!" We all laughed, which further lightened the mood.

By January 2013, Dick's private equity partners were struggling to put a real bid together. By the end of February, an alternative plan for a private investment in the publicly listed Best Buy was also dead after we failed to agree on terms. But I still wanted to find a way to work with Dick. The feud had been distracting and affected employees, many of whom knew Dick from his days as CEO. It was time to put the 10-month drama behind us and move forward.

Finally, in April, Dick Schulze agreed to rejoin the company with a new title: chairman emeritus. Although he was not rejoining the board, he agreed to provide his sage counsel to me. The Best Buy family was reunited. The war was officially over, and we could bring our talent together in service of the turnaround.

Ending with People—Always

We had to tighten our belt of course, as Best Buy's costs were bloated. But we would end with people. That means when the ship is sinking, reducing headcount comes last, not first.

This was another bit of wisdom from Jean-Marie Descarpentries, who had told me many years before that in a turnaround, the first priority is (1) to grow the top line, then (2) go after nonsalary expenses, and (3) optimize costs associated with employee benefits. If 1 + 2 + 3 is not enough, then, and only then, should cutting jobs where it makes sense be considered. This keeps people at the center of the purposeful human organization.

Some analysts had been clamoring for the blood sport—counseling Best Buy to shut down stores and slash headcount. Cut, cut, cut. But closing down stores wholesale was not the answer. I knew from previous experience how companies that end with people recover better. When I was still at Carlson, I had been inspired by how our German travel business dealt with the 2008 crisis. Corporate travel relies on sophisticated travel agents who can optimize multileg travel arrangements, navigate byzantine airline pricing, and build relationships. The recession weighed heavily on the demand for Carlson Wagonlit's services. In many markets, local management cut, cut, cut. But in Germany, thanks to local labor laws, the management team reduced working hours so everyone could keep their jobs. Senior managers also reduced their own compensation. They had no idea how long it would take for the market to recover, but they knew that keeping people was a priority. And when the market recovered, they would be ready.

The German management team was acutely aware that, when things improve, making up for the loss of expertise and experience that comes with reducing headcount when times are tough is costly. New recruits take time to find their business legs. Think of going into a Best Buy store, looking for advice. You would probably not like to speak to the newbie sales associate. You are not alone. Zero percent of customers prefer to deal with completely green employees.

I had the German division of Carlson in mind as we took on costs and tried to end with people. Here is what we did, based on Jean-Marie's playbook.

Growing the top line

The first priority was to boost revenues. Industry analysts had been predicting the death of big box retailers, blaming online competition. So, we decided to take the Amazon bull by the horns: in October 2012, ahead of the crucial holiday season, we announced that we would match online retailers' prices—including, of course, Amazon's. This would ensure that customers had no reason to showroom. We would turn the same foot traffic into more sales. We had quietly tested the idea in our Chicago stores, analyzed the results, and concluded it was worth the gamble: the boost in sales would compensate for the cost of matching prices. Our decision made a big splash.

We also revamped our website and our online shopping approach. No more "Cinderella" searches spitting out Nikon cameras. One of our most dramatic moves, initiated by Sharon McCollam, was to unlock our ability to ship online orders directly from our stores. As 70 percent of the US population lives within 10 miles of a Best Buy store, this would dramatically cut down the time it took us to deliver online purchases, which would help boost online sales.

We also worked hard to make shopping in our stores more pleasant and rewarding. We invested in the training of Blue Shirts and, as discussed in chapter 6, we began partnering with tech companies to help them showcase the fruit of their billions of dollars of R&D investments.

We also overhauled store floor plans. Growing categories like phones, tablets, and appliances expanded their footprint. Square footage for media like CDs and DVDs shrank dramatically.

Reducing nonsalary expenses

Next, we went after nonsalary costs with great intensity. We initially endeavored to eliminate $725 million in costs over several years. There was a lot we could cut, but that is still a big number. CFO Sharon McCollam applied her considerable retail experience. Improving returns, replacement, and damages alone, she figured, represented a $400 million opportunity. Televisions are a good example. Flat screens break easily and given how much they get moved around from factory to store to car to home, they break a lot. About 2 percent of our TVs ended up damaged during that journey, costing us some $180 million a year. Reducing even a fraction of that breakage would save significant costs.

We worked with manufacturers to find ways to design more damage-proof TVs and to improve packaging to better protect them, including by printing clear instructions on how to store them—standing please, not flat. We trained our warehouse and sales staff on how to handle them, and made sure these TVs were stored low, reducing the chance they would fall. We offered to deliver them to customers for free, and for those who insisted on cramming TVs in their car, we shared instructions on how to best handle the box to minimize risks.

In the same vein, we found ways to optimize product returns. Customers returned about 10 percent of what they bought from us, which

cost money and time. Take large appliances like fridges. It is not un-
common for these to get dented when they are being hauled up stairs
or around tight corners while being delivered to customers' homes. We
first gave customers better online instructions on how to measure their
space. And if what got dinged happened to be the side or the back of a
built-in fridge, for example, we gave latitude to our delivery and sales
staff to offer gift cards instead of returning an entire fridge for a minor
cosmetic damage that would become invisible once the appliance was
installed. Similarly, instead of sending back to suppliers the computers
that were being returned to us, we decided to use our broad physical
and online footprint to resell them directly—which optimized overall
recovery and earned us an allowance from manufacturers.

We also loosened rules to prevent plainly goofy, crazy, and stupid
waste. In April 2013, for example, I visited one of our return centers
in Kentucky. The place was huge, with conveyor belts churning rejects
that customers had decided they did not want after all. On one of the
belts, I spotted a green marker. A single pen that one of our stores had
sent to the return center. That pen had traveled hundreds of miles at
great expense, vastly outweighing any benefit that the return center
might extract from its recovery.

This was crazy, but the store had strictly followed policy and procedures. I took a photo of the lonely green marker and projected it at
our next meeting of store managers. I told them that if anyone on the
front line saw anything crazy, goofy, or stupid—like a green marker
being returned from a store—they should override whatever policy
was in place. If you see something, say something and do something.

Besides returns, replacement, and damages, we also paid attention
to more extravagant low-hanging fruit. Executive trips on private
planes were nixed. In January 2013, I happily walked to seat 36B in
economy class to fly to the Consumer Electronic Show. This sent a
very clear message to our vendors and our teams. At the same time,
Sharon McCollam was not going only after big-bang cost-cutting

ideas. No cost saving was too small: we turned to double-sided black and white printing instead of color. Even if it only saved marginal dollars, it set the right tone.

Optimizing employee benefits

One of our first and easiest decisions on benefits was to restore the employee discount. I had learned in St. Cloud how unpopular the decision to scrap it had been among employees. This had been hurting their morale—and therefore their willingness and ability to give their all to our turnaround. We also focused heavily on health-care costs, which typically grow by 6–8 percent a year for US employers. What could we do to optimize these costs while making sure our employees' health was still well protected? We looked closely at what was driving our health-care costs up. We established a wellness program and expanded prevention to help employees stay healthier. Once again, we collaborated with our vendors—insurance companies this time—to find solutions.

Cutting jobs as the last resort

For Best Buy, 1 + 2 + 3 did not quite add up, and we did reduce headcount. During the Renew Blue turnaround period, for example, we eliminated unnecessary management layers and shut down nonstrategic departments and initiatives—such as a service that made the Geek Squad available to other retailers. We also streamlined at the top. Anyone and everyone appeared to have a chief of staff, for example. That was not necessary.

But eliminating positions does not always mean eliminating people. In 2018, we decided to close our Best Buy mobile phone stores. It no longer made sense to have separate stores dedicated to cell phones. But I made sure that we did not run to the blanket severance package standard approach. Instead, we sent a letter to all the staff employed in these stores. The letter explained how we would assist them in any way we could to find other roles within Best Buy and sincerely hoped they would choose that option, as we valued their contribution.

There were opportunities for them. Like in most retail companies, natural staff turnover and size give us flexibility. College students who work at our stores to help pay for their studies graduate and leave. People move, or move on. Even after everything we have done to build an engaging work environment, store turnover still reaches 30 percent. It is much lower than the nearly 50 percent pre-turnaround, but it is still a lot of jobs to fill every year. Plus, we were becoming a growing business. The development of a team of in-home advisors, for example, meant new jobs were being created. We offered some of these jobs to most of our mobile store staff and worked hard to make sure that everyone felt that they could stay if they wanted to. Not everyone did—and those who left were entitled to a severance package—but we did all we could to give them that option. This is the right thing to do, because it is human *and* it makes financial sense; no place for "or" here and elsewhere. It was an easy decision to make—and to explain to shareholders.

Growing revenues, streamlining nonsalary expenses, optimizing employee benefits—these are the kind of interventions that typically do not make headlines—except for our decision to match online prices, which did make it to the newspapers. These actions are not as dramatic as slashing headcount, but they are far more effective: since 2012, Best Buy has saved about $2 billion in costs, about two-thirds of which were nonsalary expenses—far beyond the $725 million we initially targeted. The company has continued to find ways to eliminate between $200 and $300 million in costs every year. These savings have in large part been invested back into the business, making sure we continue looking after all our stakeholders.

The Renew Blue turnaround did not work in spite of our efforts to stave off workforce cuts, but instead because of it. Other measures are more effective because they make things better for customers as well as vendors and have a meaningful financial impact on the bottom line. And they are more effective because they safeguard the lifeblood of the company: the human talent, experience, dedication, and heart that constitute the core of a purposeful human organization.

Generating Human Energy

When I joined Best Buy in September 2012, the mood was grim. The company had just gone through six months of intense drama. The previous CEO had been fired, embroiled in a scandal. The interim CEO was gone as well, and now here I was, an unknown outsider stepping in. The share price was plummeting. Founder Dick Schulze had just launched his offensive to take the company private. Article after article predicted that the company would die, like consumer electronics retailer Circuit City, unable to weather market changes and low-cost online competition; in October 2012, the cover of *Bloomberg Businessweek* featured a zombie wearing a Best Buy blue shirt.

Although Best Buy had great talent and a phenomenal can-do attitude, employees were, understandably, worried and demoralized.

During a turnaround, the priority is to create the energy needed to save a dying business. It means coming up with a good plan fast; focusing everyone on clear, simple priorities; and making the environment intense but safe. It also means creating urgency with optimism, and showing fast progress, even in small steps. This is what I call "putting the organization under tension." At Best Buy, here is how we created the energy needed to turn the business around.

Cocreating a good enough, not a perfect, plan

Shortly after I started, the board of directors made it clear we needed to come up with a plan by November 1.[2] That gave us 57 days. "This is crazy!" said Maurice Levy, the CEO of Publicis, whose team was advising me on our corporate communications. He thought it could not be done and was a particularly dangerous effort.

Early in my career, when working at McKinsey, I had been trained to diagnose businesses and concoct long-term strategies. Other people would then execute these strategies. This traditional strategic planning approach, developed in the 1960s and 1970s, was still the norm. A few smart people at the top were supposed to come up with a strategy and a long-term plan, which lower echelons would then execute.

Eight weeks was indeed not enough time for that kind of approach. But that was okay with me, because beyond time, there are many problems with such an approach. For starters, it likely will fail to capture the insights of people who know in more detail what it will take to succeed. Also, people usually do not like to be told what to do if they have not been involved in creating the plan.

Our deadline did not trouble me because I also knew from previous experience that turnarounds are not about long-term planning, at least not initially. They are primarily about identifying what drives performance, about operational improvements, and—above all—about action. "Operational progress creates strategic degrees of freedom" is something I learned from the CEO of Cargill when he was on our board of directors at Carlson. We did not need a long-term strategy. We needed a plan to "stop the bleeding" and to quickly and tangibly improve our operational performance. And for that, eight weeks were enough. In eight weeks, we could at least frame the problem we had to solve, set a broad direction, and get going.

There would be no top-down grand strategy. To figure out how to save the company, everyone had to roll up their sleeves. In a series of two- or three-day workshops, about 30 of us from all parts of the business gathered around a U-shaped table in a conference room on the ground floor of Best Buy's headquarters.

Our approach? Start where Jean-Marie Descarpentries would: People → Business → Finance. We looked at the employee discount. We looked at the stores' floor plans—I had kept the napkin drawing from my visit to St. Cloud. We looked at pricing. We identified gaps and bottlenecks in our operations. During these intense workshops, I became known as the camel, turning down water and coffee breaks.

Before the deadline, we had our turnaround plan.

We still had to come up with a name for the plan. I had learned over the years that a plan needs a name to exist in the collective mind of the organization. I asked everyone to think about potential names overnight. The next day, we all chimed in and wrote 30 or so possible names on a flip chart. After putting it to a vote, we decided that "Renew Blue" sent the right message and was catchy.

Before presenting Renew Blue to investors, I ensured we had the buy-in from our broadly defined leadership group, the Best Buy Operating Council, which includes the top 150 most senior people. Unless we had everyone "all in" on it, this would not be much of a plan.

In November, we presented Renew Blue to the investment community. We introduced what we wanted to achieve for shareholders, but also for employees, customers, vendors, and the world around us. The company was in serious trouble, but our approach was to look after *all* stakeholders. No "either/or" here. No Friedman doctrine.

Our plan was not perfect, but it was good enough. Internally, it reminded everyone what we were good at, highlighted our shortcomings, and outlined a set of clear priorities around customers, employees, vendors, shareholders, and community. It delineated the path to move forward and keep us afloat.

Keeping pedaling and keeping it simple

A good plan was all we needed to create momentum and hope and get people engaged. Making decisions fast—like matching online prices and reinstating the employee discount—was crucial. It boosted people's energy and created a sense of possibility and hope. What separates great leaders from good leaders is not the quality but the quantity of decisions. More decisions create more momentum and energy. These decisions will not all be good ones. But if you know how to ride a bicycle, then you also know that it is much easier to correct course when you pedal your way forward than when you stand still.

Besides creating momentum through decisions, clarifying what is most important and keeping it simple unleashes energy; complexity creates confusion, overwhelms, and sows inertia. I knew from my visit to St. Cloud that Best Buy store managers, for example, were asked to keep their eyes on so many metrics that they could not see the forest for the trees. Imagine their reaction when they heard me say the company had only two problems: revenues were down, and margins were down. Only two problems? Not 40 KPIs? This was great news. How hard could it be to solve just two problems? Everyone had to keep their eyes, brains, and energy on these two prizes. What was standing in our way of growing revenues and growing margins? We would tackle the worst roadblocks first and then focus on the next ones.

Wait. Didn't I say earlier that focusing on numbers is not inspiring? That a company's purpose is not to make money? Yes, I did. This does not mean that you ignore numbers. Profit is an outcome, but also an imperative. When the business is dying, you have to stop the bleeding. We were doing that while also maturing into a purpose-driven company. Even back in 2012, several years before we would articulate our purpose as enriching lives through technology, we had defined our plan around all stakeholders, guided by the desire to be the preferred destination and authority when it came to technology.

While we were focusing on staying alive, measuring against these two problems (and only these two) over time would tell us whether we would survive as a business. It would allow us to keep our fingers on the pulse as we moved forward. This was how we would measure progress.

And we would identify where and who within the company was improving the most and the fastest. Then we could learn from that progress.

Creating a positive environment

The sense of urgency and clarity that contributes to putting the organization under (productive) tension comes hand in hand with creating a positive environment. No one does their best work when under severe stress or when driven by fear. Creating optimism, energy, and confidence in our future started with me. I had to be upbeat and optimistic, no matter what. When I was still at Carlson, I remember feeling drained at the end of a long day during a convention with thousands of hotel franchisees. I decided there and then that I was not tired. It was the same in those early days of Renew Blue. I get to decide how I am going to show up. Every day.

We celebrated wins any chance we got. Our communications team, headed by Matt Furman, was actively searching and sharing nuggets of good news. Look, we are growing in Chicago! And look at how well our small appliances are doing! At every team meeting and every company town hall, we highlighted what was going well. This all sent a fabulous message throughout the ranks.

We adopted the same approach with our investors. In our November 2012 presentation, we started our diagnosis by highlighting Best Buy's great strengths, such as the innovation driving growth in our consumer electronics market and the fact that we accounted for the largest single share of sales in that market. At the same time, we did not sugarcoat our operational challenges, from mediocre customer satisfaction to lackluster online performance, which weighed on financial returns.

Throughout the turnaround, we kept sharing our wins. In early 2013, for example, we tried out shipping online purchases from 50 stores.

This was a green shoot initially, with a marginal financial impact. But our CFO, Sharon McCollam, kept bringing it up in her conversations with investors, explaining why this was meaningful. Over time, the green shoot grew bigger roots as it expanded across our stores, and the initiative eventually put a major boost in online sales.

Looking on the bright side, radiating energy and celebrating wins does not mean glossing over what is not working, however. Do you remember Alan Mulally and his system of red-amber-green lights? Ford was facing bankruptcy, but all the lights were green. To save a company, bad news has to travel at least as fast as good news. You cannot solve problems if you do not know where they are.

Being positive and acknowledging challenges are both necessary, and neither can dominate. When we were working through our Renew Blue plan, one of our bright staff in the strategy department produced a 300-page PowerPoint deck highlighting all the familiar issues and challenges we had to address. The presentation concluded that Best Buy was doomed. If you are not able to turn challenges into possibilities and silver linings, then you have no business leading a turnaround. I decided to ignore the PowerPoint presentation's gloomy prediction.

Being transparent and encouraging vulnerability

When preparing our Renew Blue turnaround plan, we had faced a dilemma. Should we keep it under wraps until the investor presentation in November 2012? Or should we share it within the company, get feedback, and make sure that everyone was all in? Best Buy is a listed company, and any leak to the media would have affected the share price. Should we choose to be fearful and suspicious? Or should we trust our people? Our executive team was split. There had been damaging leaks to the media in the past. But I believed that the risk of leak was far smaller than taking the risk that our people would not own the turn-around plan. Three weeks before the investor presentation, we gathered 150 of our managers and shared our draft plan. We made it very clear that what we were about to share and discuss was highly confidential. We got valuable feedback and buy-in, and there was zero leak.

Throughout the turnaround, we discussed openly within Best Buy and with our shareholders our situation, our priorities, our opportunities, our challenges, our progress, and our "say/do" ratio. This energized our teams and promoted accountability.

I was not afraid to ask for help either. Three months after I became CEO, I brought in my coach, Marshall Goldsmith. Deep into our turnaround, I asked my team for feedback. I shared with them what I wanted to be better at, which included becoming better at delegating. I did not pretend to have all the answers or to be perfect. I asked for help—and received it—from my very first days at Best Buy, whether working in the St. Cloud store or with the executive team.

We had to do the same as a company. We had to leverage other people's strengths and look for partners if we wanted to survive. This is how we collaborated with our vendors, as we talked about in chapter 6. This is why we asked other suppliers, such as Accenture, IBM, and UPS, for temporary discounts. We were not afraid to ask for help. And we got it.

This signaled within the company that no one should be afraid to be vulnerable. No one should be afraid to ask for help. No one should feel he or she had to pretend to be invincible or perfect, because we are all human, and it is in our vulnerability that we connect and unlock the power of the collective. This is how we connect with each other. This is how we connect with our customers, suppliers, communities, and shareholders. This is what a purposeful human organization is made of—in sickness and in health, in good times and in bad ones.

. . .

In January 2013, just a couple of months into Renew Blue, we reported sales for November and December 2012. The preceding quarter's results had been a disaster, but we had excellent news to announce: compared to the previous year, our sales were flat.

Flat sales! We were thrilled! It was far better than the slump analysts expected. It suggested that we had stopped the hemorrhage. The market was blown away, and the share price started to recover. We had turned a corner. The change of mood within Best Buy was palpable. We kept going with our turnaround plan, feeling a pleasant wind at our backs.

To this day, many Best Buy employees tell me that the few years of our Renew Blue turnaround were one of the best times of their professional lives. We were on a mission together, and the energy was electrifying. Together we navigated the storm and were exhilarated as we defied all expectations. We were supposed to die. But even now, people who went through it still remember that we had only two problems, and we solved them.

What happened at Best Buy during Renew Blue is what I call "human magic." It is what happens when each individual within the company is fired up and when everyone working together achieves more than they ever thought possible. Human magic results in irrational—irrationally good—performance.

Successfully building a purposeful human organization—whether in good times or in a turnaround—requires unleashing that kind of energy.

We unleash this human magic by creating a daily work environment where every individual can feel engaged and all-in. That is what part three is all about.

Questions to Reflect On

What is your approach to dealing with people during difficult times?

People first:

- How do you stay connected with the front line?

- What is your approach to building the right senior team?

People last:

- How do you tend to prioritize revenue growth and cost reduction?

- What are the best results you have seen in attacking nonsalary expenses and creatively managing benefits?

Generating human energy:

- What do you do to create energy?

- To what degree and how do you engage others in the development of the plan?

- What do you do to create a positive environment? How well is this working?

- How do you decide how you will show up at work every day?

- How transparent do you like to be? What approach do you use to communicate broadly?

Generally:

- What approach do you find particularly effective to drive performance in a turnaround situation?

- What would you like to become better at? What areas are you working on?

Part Three

UNLEASHING
HUMAN MAGIC

The old approach to management—having a few smart people formulate a strategy, craft an elaborate implementation plan, communicate the plan to everyone else, and put in place incentives to mobilize people around the plan—rarely works. After discussing in part one why we work, and defining companies as purposeful human organizations in part two, we present in part three an alternative to that outdated management approach. We lay out the ingredients that unleash what I call *human magic*. By creating an environment where everyone at the company is energized in support of a great cause, these ingredients drive engagement and, when coupled with a sound strategy, result in extraordinary performance. This is the human dimension that powers corporations as purposeful human organizations.

8

Moving Past Carrots and Sticks

The carrot and the stick are pervasive and persuasive motivators. But if you treat people like donkeys, they will perform like donkeys.

—John Whitmore, *Coaching for Performance, GROWing Human Potential and Purpose*

In 1986, Dick Schulze, Best Buy's founder, was facing a serious challenge. The business he had started 20 years earlier was under attack from Detroit-based consumer electronics chain Highland Superstores. Highland, the second largest electronics retailer in the United States, had opened stores in Best Buy's own turf of Minneapolis and was selling at rock bottom, unsustainable prices.

Best Buy had been close to bankruptcy twice before, and this was another critical life-or-death moment. Dick felt that Highland, a much larger company that could afford to take losses for a time, was doing everything it could to run Best Buy out of business.

In crisis mode, Dick zoomed in on one question: How could Best Buy change the playing field? The answer seemed to be getting rid of "spiffs"—bonuses paid by suppliers to salespeople who pushed their products.

Dick wanted sales associates to focus on giving the best, most objective advice possible to customers. That was difficult with spiffs. At the time, spiffs were central to salespeople's compensation at Best Buy and elsewhere. Unsurprisingly, customers hated spiffs, even if they might not know the word itself. They felt that salespeople pushed brands that offered the highest commissions, regardless of whether these products were what shoppers needed.

Dick had the idea to abolish commissions and pay Blue Shirts by the hour instead but, he says, "it was almost heresy to ask it, let alone think it."[1] The risk was sizable. Back then, half of Best Buy's 1,000 employees worked on commission and had done so for their entire careers. This was just how sales were done, a system no one questioned. Dick did not want to undermine the company spirit; disrupt store operations; or, worst of all, antagonize employees. Best Buy might lose its best Blue Shirts.

At the same time, ending spiffs would benefit customers, which could set Best Buy apart from its competition. Blue Shirts would become facilitators rather than the suppliers' de facto agents. Inventory would move from hidden backrooms to the store floor, where all customers could see what was available. The stores themselves would become more like warehouses, with cement floors, metal racks, and fluorescent lighting—big boxes where the focus would not be pushing specific brands, but providing customers value.

Staff bonuses would reflect store or district performance—not individual achievement. At the same time, salespeople who wanted to become managers would be offered a career path of promotion from within, with higher base salaries.

By 1988, Dick was ready to test the idea, known as Concept II, in seven new stores opening in the Midwest. It worked. Sales in the new concept stores were high enough that Concept II expanded to other locations. Eventually, those stores doubled the sales of the commission-based stores.

Dick's gamble paid off. Concept II saved Best Buy and propelled it to many years of high performance. In 1999, when I first got to know Best Buy as a vendor during my years leading Vivendi Games, it struck me then as the most sophisticated and most customer-focused consumer electronics company around, powered by great people.

And Highland Superstores? The company went out of business.

What Dick Schulze realized before most of us did was that, in today's economy, financial incentives do not drive performance. The carrot-and-stick approach is in fact often counterproductive. Financial incentives still have a role to play—as long as they are not expected to motivate people.

Financial Incentives No Longer Drive Performance

Surprisingly, financial incentives are still used, broadly, to motivate people. Human resources teams around the world spend an inordinate amount of time, resources, and brain power to design and manage such incentive programs.

I too believed in the money-as-motivator system for much of my professional life. One of my first decisions as the CEO of Carlson Companies, in 2008, was to help design a long-term incentive plan for senior management, tied to the value we were hoping to create, as a way to mobilize the organization around economic performance.

Then in 2015, I came across an animation created around a Daniel Pink presentation on what motivates us.[2] Pink cites a study conducted at the Massachusetts Institute of Technology (MIT) that gave various mental puzzles and physical challenges to a group of students. To incentivize the students' performance, three levels of cash prizes were offered, based on how well they did. When tasks involved even rudimentary cognitive skills, the larger reward led to poorer performance.

The result was so puzzling that the economists who conducted the study decided to repeat the experiment. Perhaps the cash rewards they had offered were not enticing enough to motivate MIT students. In rural India, on the other hand, the same top cash reward was equivalent to two months' salary. But the results held.

Economists, psychologists, and sociologists have replicated these results many times, and the more sophisticated and creative the task is, the more counterproductive incentives are. They tend to narrow our focus and our minds. And for complex, creative tasks, we need exactly the opposite: the more we can expand our mind and think outside the proverbial box, the better we do.[3]

Listening to Daniel Pink, I nearly fell off my chair. These results, backed by further research, went against all I had been taught. It negated the rationale for the incentives carefully crafted by every company where I had worked, many of which I'd helped design. How could this be? Isn't our good old capitalist system based on the belief that we are supposed to be driven by money?

Over time, though, I have embraced this idea as nearly common sense. I even test it sometimes. Recently, I had dinner with a fellow CEO and asked him if he thought financial incentives drive performance.

"Of course they do!" he exclaimed.

Then I asked him if financial incentives drove him, personally, to perform at his best.

"Of course they don't!"

If financial incentives do not motivate us personally, why would we think they motivate others? I now believe financial incentives are:

- Outdated

- Misguided

- Potentially dangerous and poisonous

- Hard to get right in any event

Let me elaborate.

Financial incentives are outdated as they were designed for a different type of work

Frederick Taylor based his approach of scientific management on the premise that, as work was a tedious and unenjoyable means to an end (see chapter 2), the only way to motivate an otherwise unmotivated workforce was money. Indeed, the narrowing of focus that incentives bring about, though terrible for innovation and lateral thinking, helps speed up simple tasks.

Taylor's perspective greatly shaped remuneration and broader management practices for much of the twentieth century. Long-term strategic planning, developed in the 1960s and 1970s, is rooted in a similar view of the world: that workers need carrots and sticks to execute a strategy designed by smart executives with the help of expert staffers, and then translated into a plan, cascading goals, aligned financial incentives, and a system of control and compliance that measures how well people perform against these goals.

Businesses have therefore built entire systems of financial incentives, bonuses, commissions, and other financial rewards to motivate their employees. The problem, though, is that work has changed.

Financial incentives are misguided, as they are focused on compliance rather than engagement

Even when rewards are linked to repetitive tasks, in which case they appear to motivate more and faster production, they have serious limitations. Neither carrots nor sticks are very good at changing human behavior over long periods of time—let alone permanently. Rewards and punishments are what psychologists label as "extrinsic motivators," which do not fundamentally drive or change behavior, whether it is trying to lose weight, stop smoking, or change how you work.

Drive and engagement at work come from a flame that burns from within; carrots and sticks do not create it. In fact, they actively snuff it out.[4]

Financial incentives can be dangerous and poisonous

When I was president of EDS France, EDS landed a contract with the subsidiary of a large French chain of grocery stores. The deal looked like it would generate millions of dollars of revenue, which was a major coup. Unfortunately, the team underestimated the challenges and overestimated the company's ability to deliver on its promises. We eventually managed to get the project done, but we lost money on that contract. Given the nature of the business, it took years to realize that the initial financial projections would not materialize.

In retrospect, I think EDS's incentive system contributed to the problem. The sales team's hefty commission for landing the deal was based on the estimated value of the contract they brought in. This encourages salespeople to make enthusiastic promises and projections that are not necessarily realistic.

In this way, incentives can become poisonous. Dangle pay-for-performance in front of people, and they also become tempted to hide mistakes or shortcomings, rather than seek help and see challenges as chances to learn and grow. Pushed even further, incentives may result in plain wrongdoing.

In addition, efforts to appeal to self-interested and ethical motivations at the same time often fail, because incentives send the signal that we act out of self-interest, undermining what Adam Smith called "the moral sentiments."[5]

Financial incentives are hard to get right

Many companies and leaders continue to spend an inordinate amount of time and resources trying to design the perfect incentive system. I certainly did on many occasions in the last 30 years, first as a management consultant and then as CEO and/or board member of multiple companies in a variety of industries.

Yet sophisticated, supposedly resilient systems quickly become irrelevant when the environment changes. When I was at privately owned Carlson, the human resources team and I labored to produce a system that would mirror what existed in publicly listed companies. In 2008, the incentives plan was launched. A few months later, the recession sank the carefully crafted plan.

There is also the challenge of time horizons. Businesses operating on long cycles, from aircraft manufacturers to energy and pharma companies, face a disconnect between management tenure and when results show up. Incentives are paid based on annual or at best triannual results, but these results mostly reflect decisions made 5, 10, or even 15 years earlier.

What Incentives Are For

Despite all this, incentives can still be useful—as long as we stop believing that they can motivate and mobilize an organization. Bonuses tied to company performance, for example, are a useful tool to share good financial times with employees—not just shareholders. Incentives can also signal what is most important. At EDS France, I changed the company's bonus system, which had to that point been based on financial results only. I wanted to make it clear that when I said "people, business, finance"—in that order—I meant it. The new bonuses were calculated based on these three measures, which were given equal weight:

1. A "people" component, including metrics such as turnover, engagement, and whether performance appraisals were conducted, and conducted on time

2. A "business" tranche that reflected how well we did on customer satisfaction, churn, and the like

3. A financial portion, based on the results of the company

"Are you sure you really want to do this?" asked David Thorpe, who ran EDS's business in Europe, the Middle East, and Africa. He was concerned that bonuses may be paid out even when financial performance was poor. I told him I was not worried. If we did well on people and business, then the financial results would follow. Introducing new metrics into the system would ensure that the "people" and "business" elements received more attention. The new incentive system served as an effective loudspeaker.

When I joined Best Buy in 2012, the top echelons of the company were heavily siloed. We urgently needed to have everyone focused on the whole rather than their parts, so we changed the bonus system to send a clear signal. Everyone on the management team would receive the same bonus based on how Best Buy performed as a whole. How the incentive was calculated also clearly reminded everyone of our priorities during our Renew Blue turnaround plan (chapter 7): growing the top line, boosting e-commerce, improving customer satisfaction, and reducing costs accounted for a sizable part of the measurement.

Not for a second did we believe that anyone would jump out of bed in the morning because of those bonuses, devising while driving to work how to best maximize the payout. So yes, Best Buy had—and still has—an incentive system. But it is not meant to motivate. It is meant to communicate and to share the benefits of the outcome.

. . .

If incentives do not motivate people to go the extra mile, then what will? What unleashes the human magic that powers the purposeful human organization laid out in part two?

It starts with one fundamental change of perspective: to view people as a *source* rather than a resource. Employees must be treated as individuals working together in pursuit of a common purpose, rather than as an "asset." Each employee is an individual with his or her own motivations and sense of purpose, not human capital driven exclusively by money. It is time to move past the quest to drive the behavior of a collective workforce, and instead seek to inspire people by connecting with what matters to each one of them. Unleashing human magic means creating an environment in which *individuals* flourish. Because when people are doing what matters to them and what they believe in, they will walk through walls, pouring their energy, creativity, and emotions into their job.

Best Buy and its people have taught me much about the practical implications of this shift in perspective. I believe the recipe for creating that environment is in fact made of five key ingredients:

- Connecting individual search for meaning with the company's noble purpose

- Developing authentic human connections

- Fostering autonomy

- Growing mastery

- Nurturing a growth environment

The following chapters explore each of these ingredients.

Questions to Reflect On

- Do you believe that financial incentives motivate people to perform better? Do they motivate you?

- How are incentives used in your company? What priorities do they reflect?

- What drives you?

9

First Ingredient: Connecting Dreams

Tutor 1: What does it feel like when you're dancing?

Billy: Don't know. Sorta feels good. Sorta stiff and that, but once I get going . . . then I like, forget everything. And . . . sorta disappear. Sorta disappear. Like I feel a change in my whole body. And I've got this fire in my body. I'm just there. Flyin' like a bird. Like electricity. Yeah, like electricity.

—Billy Elliot

"What is your dream?"

Jason Luciano, the manager at the South Bay Best Buy store in Dorchester, south of Boston, asked every single person on his team this question. Every associate's answer was written on a whiteboard in the break room, next to their name. After writing it down, Jason would always tell them, "Let's work together to help you achieve it."

I visited the South Bay store in 2016, around the outset of the Building the New Blue growth plan. Nobody knew I was coming. Impromptu visits like this helped me stay connected to the front line and to what was happening in stores. As Shari Ballard, Best Buy's phenomenal president of retail until 2019, wisely pointed out to me a few years ago, we could not lead a company like Best Buy from a spreadsheet in our offices.

I knew before my visit that South Bay was performing well. I was keen to find out what they were doing that other stores could learn from. It turns out that the simple question, "What is your dream?" and what Jason, inspired by the district manager who had introduced this approach in the area, did with each answer explained much of the store's success. By figuring out what drove every person on his team, he truly connected with each one of them. But his real genius was then to find a way to link their dreams with the company's purpose.

He told me about a Blue Shirt whose dream was to be able to move into her own apartment. What fundamentally drove her was to find independence. If she remained on an hourly wage in the mobile-phone department, it would be difficult to afford her own place. Together, they drew a plan for her to become a supervisor or assistant manager. What would it take? What skills did she need to develop to get these promotions? And how could he help her get there?

With the support of her manager and the team, the young woman grew in confidence, helped improve the performance of her unit, and became someone who inspired her colleagues. When a position to lead the computing department opened up, she got it. Eventually, she fulfilled her dream and got her own apartment.

The store manager's commitment to help every member of his team achieve their dream was extraordinary, and incredible to witness up close. It gave teams the energy that, combined with their skills, drove the store's superior performance. Enriching the lives of customers through technology enabled employees to enrich their own lives, as store managers helped them see how this related to their own dream, whatever it happened to be. They understood that purpose and human connections—between store manager and everyone on the team, as well as between Blue Shirts and their colleagues, customers, suppliers, communities, and shareholders—are at the heart of business.

Getting invested in what the company stands for because it reso- nates with what makes you get out of bed in the morning is one of the essential ingredients of engagement. Clearly articulating and feeding that connection between personal and company purpose for every team member is therefore one of the most crucial roles of any leader, from top executives to store managers. It is like the electricity that Billy Elliot, the miner's young son in the 2000 movie of the same name, talks about when asked what it feels like when he is dancing. If, like me, you were schooled in data and analytics, this might feel squishy. Early in my career, I would have agreed with you. But it works. It is the kind of connection that I have witnessed at Best Buy and seen produce what some would characterize as an improbable miracle. This is what creates "love brands" and an enduring emotional bond and loyalty between a business and the people whose lives it touches.

Humanity is what binds personal to collective purpose. Most people want to do something good for others. When a company strives to do good things and help people, the connection between personal drive and the company's noble purpose is easy to make.

An increasing number of businesspeople agree. But *how* does it work in practice? How do we foster that connection and nurture it?

For us at Best Buy, it took an iterative process that continues today and entails the following:

- Explicitly articulating the people-first philosophy

- Exploring what drives people around you

- Capturing moments that matter

- Sharing stories and encouraging role modeling

- Framing the company's purpose in a meaningful, human, and authentic fashion

- Spreading meaning

Explicitly Articulating the People-First Philosophy

On Monday, August 20, 2012, the day that my appointment as CEO of Best Buy was announced, I addressed 500 or so directors and officers of the company gathered at headquarters. Of course, I told them how excited I was to be joining Best Buy, and shared my views about the business and my confidence that, together, we could turn around the company. I also shared with them my management philosophy around people, business, and finance—in that order—with profit being an outcome and an imperative, not the goal. I laid bare my belief that the purpose of a company is not to make money, but to make a positive contribution in people's lives.

Articulating these views early and often is important, so they take root, grow throughout the organization, and create a fertile ground for everyone to flourish.

Shari Ballard was excellent at telling our 125,000 employees that every person counts. She forcefully and repeatedly made the point that the size of the company makes no difference: we touch the lives of people one at a time. Shari would encourage our store managers and our Blue Shirts to look at customers the way they look at their family and their friends. How would you help your mom and dad choose a new TV? Or your sister? "I fell in love with the company in the first place, and still love it, because at the core, it's an entirely human business," she said. "We are people working together to serve other people in support of a mission that matters in people's lives."

Every significant meeting for the past few years has highlighted that individuals and their journey are at the core of the business. That sense of personal purpose, as well as Best Buy's mission to enrich lives of customers through technology, is central to every gathering. "I am Best Buy" was the theme of the 2019 Holiday Leadership Meeting, which focused on how every individual's story contributes to the fabric of the company.

In March 2020, shortly after I announced that I would be stepping down as executive chairman of the company and almost eight years after that first town hall meeting, I received a message from an in-home advisor in California. Arnie thanked me for articulating throughout my years at Best Buy the value of being yourself, serving others, and finding your purpose. He told me it had helped him, not only at work but more generally in life. His words of gratitude touched me very deeply of course. They also made me realize that being clear about these beliefs had touched more people than I realized.

Exploring What Drives People around You

We saw how this worked at the South Bay store in Boston. But I have experienced other examples. The executive team retreat during which we each shared formative stories from our lives and what motivated us connected us to each other and deepened our understanding of the link between us and the company's mission. I also remember when Marilyn Carlson Nelson interviewed me for the job of CEO at Carlson. "Tell me about your soul," she said. She wanted to know what motivated me and whether it aligned with the company's purpose and values. I shared what I had gotten out of the Loyola exercises, the importance of my spiritual life, how I had evolved over time, and my views on profit and the purpose of corporations. We were on a nine-hour flight from Paris to Minneapolis, which gave us plenty of time to explore the question.

After decades of "mean business" as the dominant corporate credo, it is time to push for mean*ing* in business, and this starts with every individual's own sense of purpose and how or whether it aligns with the company's purpose.

Capturing Moments That Matter

During my time as CEO of Best Buy, few moments were as meaningful and impactful as when Hurricane Maria devastated Puerto Rico.

From the mainland, it was initially hard to fathom the extent of the devastation. The storm had knocked out the island's electrical and communications infrastructure. Homes were blown apart or flooded beyond repair. Roads were impassable. Hospitals were inaccessible or evacuated. The morning after the storm, Davian Altamiranda, the Florida-based district manager responsible for Puerto Rico, did not know any of that yet, and he dutifully phoned into his scheduled 9 a.m. conference call with the managers of our three stores in Puerto Rico—a call the managers never missed. When no one else made it onto the call, Davian worried. Best Buy had a total of about 300 employees on the island in our stores and our distribution center, and we could not locate any of them at first. Where were they? Were they okay?

Our team sprang into action. First, we had to find a way to contact everybody to make sure they were safe. In some cases, we asked employees to find their colleagues and put the word out in the community that we needed to know if everyone was okay. Little by little, we were able to account for everyone. But that did not mean they were all right. Some had lost their homes and all their possessions, and they did not have enough food and clean water to survive. One Best Buy employee, who was seven months pregnant and type 1 diabetic, had lost the electricity required to keep her medications cool. We could see on television that loads of relief supplies were en route to the island, but our folks in Puerto Rico told us they were not seeing any of those supplies. They were getting desperate.

Davian Altamiranda called Amber Cales, Best Buy's vice president responsible for the Southeast region. "We have to do something," he said.

"What are you thinking?" Amber replied. Ports were not open.

"I need a cargo plane!" Davian said.

"Okay," she replied without hesitation. "Let's see what we can do."

Amber got to work. "How do I hire a private plane?" she asked her boss. "Do I charge it on my credit card?"

A few days later, Davian and his team arrived with the first shipment of emergency supplies. More than 200 employees, many wearing their Best Buy blue jerseys, were waiting to greet them at our San Juan store. An emotional Davian stood on a makeshift platform in the store and told the employees that we had not forgotten about them.

Every employee was handed $200 to buy emergency supplies. We continued to pay our workers for four weeks after the storm, even though the stores were closed, starting with a $1,000 advance to provide a short-term financial buffer. We then continued to pay any employee who volunteered in the community to help rebuild the island. The plane returned to the mainland with 70 people—employees and their families who chose to evacuate. We reassigned them to jobs in our local Florida stores.

All told, the plane made 14 trips to Puerto Rico, filled with supplies of diapers, water, and food; and seven trips to take employees to the mainland, including our pregnant diabetic colleague. Over time, we helped our people piece their lives back together. And they, in turn, helped Best Buy do the same.

Three months after the hurricane, more than a hundred shoppers lined up in front of Best Buy's newly repaired San Juan store before the doors opened. A band played an upbeat tune for a ribbon-cutting celebration. The first customers walking through the doors were greeted with wild applause from our staff. Under other circumstances, the store's opening might have been a sign of failure: it had missed the Black Friday holiday sales kickoff.

But I could not have been happier. That we were open for business a mere three months after Hurricane Maria was a case study in resilience and purpose. Within a year, all three stores and our distribution facility on the island were open again. Remarkably, our year-on-year sales in each of those locations soared 10 to 15 percent.

The business outcome happens to be extraordinary. But in my mind, how our company's employees helped each other through the trauma of losing everything overnight is the real achievement. What our team accomplished in Puerto Rico is one of the things I am most proud of in all my years as CEO of Best Buy—particularly because I had little to do with it. This was about people pulling together. "We are serious when we say this is a family," Amber Cales said. "If you wear this Blue Shirt, we are going to help you and it doesn't matter how." For Davian Altamiranda, helping out when people need it is the very spirit of Best Buy.

Capturing the moment amplified its effect. At the following Holiday Leadership Meeting, we showed a video about the ordeal, seen through the eyes of our people in Puerto Rico and those on the mainland who had organized support. We wanted to make sure that we communicated the essence of who we were and wanted to be as an organization. The story of what we had actually done as Best Buy crystallized our purpose for everyone. We had always said that people came first. Telling the story of Puerto Rico showed that these were not just words. Our people also saw the face—many faces in fact—of our purpose in action. It became a platform we could build on.

Sharing Stories and Encouraging
Role Modeling

Our brains are wired to connect through storytelling. Narrative gives us a sense of shared experience and humanity. We naturally find meaning and inspiration in stories. Telling everyday stories—stories of employees, customers, communities, and how they impact each other's lives—fosters a sense of purpose and connection with where we work and whom we work with.

There are easy ways to do this in any company. Best Buy's blog collects and publishes stories. Blue Shirts performing surgery on broken toy dinosaurs (chapter 3); employees helping homeless veterans and families left destitute by the fires in California; fathers and sons both wearing Blue Shirts. These are more examples of connecting purpose to practice.

I find that role modeling helps too. Explicitly sharing experiences of meaningful work and articulating the connection with the company's purpose fosters a sense of shared meaning within an organization.[1] It also creates a fertile and nurturing environment for people to identify their own purpose, and signals that this is something important. Even now, deep into the "Building the New Blue" growth campaign at Best Buy, role modeling starts every meeting. People tell their own personal story of change, why it matters to them, and how Best Buy and the company's purpose fit into it.

Our company get-togethers are full of human stories of purpose told from the stage or from the screen. There is the executive who explained at the Holiday Meeting in 2019 how and why the relationships he forged throughout his 24-year career at Best Buy had given him a sense of purpose, starting with the store manager who had "flipped the switch" in his 18-year-old self. There is the hearing-impaired customer we saw in a video who was so thankful we had hired a Blue Shirt who knew sign language. There is the story of the in-home advisor who changed the life of a disabled woman by installing voice-activated light switches and door locks around her house.

This may seem like corporate propaganda. But these stories keep reminding everyone at Best Buy of the company's purpose, how every employee contributes to it, and the difference it makes in people's lives. Maintaining that connection is crucial to engagement.

Framing the Company's Purpose in a Meaningful, Human, and Authentic Fashion

Medtronic, the medical equipment company based in Minnesota, provides a clear example of a company framing its purpose in a meaningful and authentic fashion. The company was led for many years by my friend and neighbor Bill George, who authored *Discover Your True North*.[2] Medtronic's mission, written in 1960, is focused on transforming people's lives by alleviating their pain, restoring their health, and extending their lives through the application of biomedical engineering. In case Medtronic's employees ever lose sight of this purpose, they can just look at the company's logo, a human body rising from lying down to standing.

Framing a meaningful and authentic purpose is not limited to companies engaged in the business of saving lives. "Meaningful" is about making a difference in people's lives in a way that matters to employees. "Authentic" is about credibility—something aligned with what the company does, that it is able to deliver, and that is at the core of its DNA. When I was at Carlson Wagonlit Travel, for example, we helped our clients reduce their carbon footprint by comparing the impact of various modes of transportation. Although this was meaningful, the ultimate contradiction with our business undermined its authenticity: the optimal reduction would have been cutting travel altogether, thereby killing the company.

As discussed in chapter 6, Best Buy's resurgence has a lot to do with defining the company's purpose—to enrich lives through technology by addressing key human needs—and translating it into daily behaviors across the company. Best Buy's purpose did not come from communication consultants dreaming up a clever formulation on a PowerPoint slide. It was developed organically, in part by observing who we were when we were at our best, as described earlier. This gives it genuine and deep-rooted authenticity.

I also admire how Ralph Lauren's purpose of "inspiring the dream of a better life" is a case study in authenticity—a feeling that only deepened when I visited Ralph and his wife, Ricky, in Colorado. I already knew how much that purpose was rooted in his own life story: the son of Jewish immigrants from Belarus who grew up in the Bronx, Ralph has designed clothing and home lines that reflect his own vision of the ultimate American dream, from the preppy and athletic look of the Polo line to the quintessential American cowboy. This is a dream that genuinely inspired the boy from modest origins to shape his life with spectacular success. Staying at his Colorado home further confirmed that authenticity. This rustic working ranch is a pure extension of Ralph Lauren the man. It is warm and welcoming, and nothing feels staged or forced, from antique planks repurposed from old Montana barns to tepees hand painted by Native American artists. "Inspiring the dream of a better life" is not an empty slogan. It is the core of who Ralph Lauren is and what he believes in, and everyone who works at his company knows it, feels it, and is inspired by it.

When your clients are companies, finding the connection with your own purpose is not that different. Ultimately, these companies also affect people's lives. When I was at EDS, for example, all our clients were businesses. But these businesses themselves served individuals.

This became very clear to everyone when we worked on the IT systems that would help broadcast the soccer World Cup to millions of fans around the world. This project energized not only the team but the entire organization.

Spreading Meaning

Finally, cascading meaning throughout operations and into policies helps connect individuals and what matters to them with the company's purpose. This can be done even in unexpected places: Best Buy injected meaning into its code of ethics in 2019. Typically, these codes are written by lawyers as rules detailing the many ways you could get fired. They are defensive, listing what you should *not* do.

I worked closely with our compliance team in 2018 to breathe life into the code. Instead of austere policies couched in legalese, we came up with an interactive document meant to help each of us be "at our best" for every decision, every day.

The new code starts by listing the company's beliefs, purpose, guiding behaviors, and values—the compass that guides each of us through sticky situations. The code focuses on intentions, worded in positive and simple terms, and is articulated around customers, employees, vendors, shareholders, and communities. The document does get into more details. Guidance around customers, for example, covers advertising, product safety, and data privacy, but dos and don'ts are linked to the company's purpose and values. The idea is not to cover every possible situation—no document ever could—but to encourage people to use good intent and judgment. Kamy Scarlett, who succeeded Shari Ballard as Best Buy's president of retail in 2019, best captured this approach when she told store managers that SOP did not stand for "standard operating procedures," but for "service over policy." It is up to everyone in the company, knowing our purpose and philosophy, to do what makes sense.

. . .

Creating the conditions for each and every employee to feel personally invested in the company's purpose because it resonates with what drives them is the first ingredient of human magic. That connection is steeped in making a difference in other people's lives, which is directly related to our second ingredient: creating authentic human connections.

Questions to Reflect On

- Are you clear about what drives you?

- How does your own sense of purpose connect with your company's?

- Do you know what drives each member of your team? What gives each member energy?

- How are you working with your team members to achieve their purpose?

- How do you help connect what drives people around you to the company's purpose?

10

Second Ingredient: Developing Human Connections

All I know for certain, . . . Is love is all there is.

—Sheryl Crow

When Kamy Scarlett, then Best Buy's head of human resources, shared a story, she did not hold back: "I spent the last 10 years not telling anyone about my depression because I didn't want the label or judgment or, worse still, the sympathy I believed would come from others," she wrote on the company blog, shining a light on mental health and wellness. She shared how she had struggled with severe depression after brain cancer took both her parents within six months of each other. To cope, she lost herself in work and in busyness, cutting herself off from friends and family, until her husband Mike nudged her to seek help. She went to therapy and took medication. Her depression gradually lifted, and she trains her mind every day to keep it at bay. "The shadow cast by others gave me the courage to share," she wrote. "In the spirit of paying it forward, I am hoping the shadow created by my story brings courage to you."

Kamy unleashed a flood of support from Best Buy employees. Many people saw themselves in her experience and connected with it—and with her. Hundreds responded to her post. Kamy also received 371 personal e-mails, each with a personal story. During one of her store visits, a young woman told her she had tried to commit suicide. After reading Kamy's blog post, she got help.

Chapter 9 discussed how connecting individual purpose with the company's feeds the kind of profound engagement that results in extraordinary performance. The second ingredient is to create an environment in which connections can blossom—the way they did between Kamy and her colleagues.

Human Connections Drive Engagement and Performance

Question 10 in Gallup's engagement survey is "Do you have a best friend at work?" I first heard about that question when I was working at Carlson Wagonlit Travel, and I was skeptical. This sounded too fluffy and soft to be of much value. I had been schooled in Cartesian rigor, science, and math. Data. Throughout my years at McKinsey, EDS, Vivendi, and Carlson Wagonlit Travel, I believed that effective leadership was mostly about intellect, rationality, hard work—and yes, being nice as well. But what would having a best friend at work have to do with performance?

Yet it was at Carlson that, slowly, I began to see that best friends at work may be valuable after all.

When I moved from Carlson Wagonlit Travel, Carlson still owned hotel and restaurant franchise businesses. In a restaurant franchise like TGI Friday's, every restaurant had the same strategic positioning, the same decor, and the same menu. But performance across outlets varied greatly.

What explained the difference in performance was the human factor. How the general manager related to staff informed how staff connected with customers. I saw that when managers created an environment where everyone felt they belonged and mattered, employees gave their best. By the time I joined Best Buy in 2012, I had transformed my position on Gallup question 10. Ultimately, people do not give their best because they are blown away by superior intellect. How much of themselves they invest in their work is directly related to how much they feel respected, valued, and cared for, which happens to be what friends do for each other.

We cannot exist without connecting with others. In fact, a study has identified that human connections are one of the reasons why people in Blue Zones—five areas around the world, including Okinawa, Japan, and Sardinia, Italy—live a longer and better life.[1] Human connections, in this context, include a sense of belonging, putting family first—parents, partners, and children—and supportive social circles. Okinawans, for example, have something known as *moais*, which are groups of close lifelong friends.

The basic need for human connection became strikingly apparent during the Covid-19 crisis. Besides the explosion of virtual connections through technology during self-isolation and lockdowns, people in places like China and Italy took to singing and playing music from their balconies to remind everyone around them that they were not alone and ease the sense of solitary confinement, which has a significant impact on mental health.

My new conviction in connections at work influenced how I approached my first Holiday Leadership Meeting at Best Buy. With margins and revenues eroding, and our turnaround plan still being formulated, analysts were writing our obituary. I do not remember exactly what I said on that day. If you asked anyone who was there, few would probably recall my words. But I suspect many could tell you what they felt as they listened: hope and confidence, combined with realism and urgency. They remember my tone and energy. I was upbeat and optimistic, and honest too. Everyone in that room felt invigorated but also understood that the analysts were right: if Best Buy did not change, the company would die.

As I stepped down as CEO, and later as executive chairman, it became even more evident to me that my colleagues will not remember how smart I may be or how we executed some plan. What people remember is how I made them feel. What comes through from the heartwarming messages I've received is a sense of hope and energy and inspiration.

Although it is now clear to me that human connections are essential to engagement, they're still not something that business schools and boardrooms think about or talk about much. This must change, as human magic, in the context of an effective strategy, leads to exceptional performance.

. . .

I understood *why* human connections mattered when I started at Best Buy, but it was during my years as CEO that I learned about *how* to create them. My former colleague Shari Ballard often said that companies are not soulless entities; they are human organizations made of individuals working together toward a common purpose. To unleash human magic, everyone must feel at home, fully valued for who they are, with the space and freedom to be themselves. Only then can people bring their best selves at work. Such environments get created by enacting the following:

- Fostering respect by treating everyone as an individual

- Creating a safe and transparent environment to build trust

- Encouraging vulnerability

- Developing effective team dynamics

- Ensuring diversity and inclusion

This has become a pillar of Best Buy's strategic transformation and its soul as a company.

Treating Everyone as an Individual

"Make people feel they are big," said Shari Ballard—a notion I wholeheartedly embrace. And you do this in a large company the same way you would in a small business. Typically, in any company, a general manager has 5 to 10 direct reports and directly interacts with a few dozen people. This was true for me at EDS France, which had 3,000 employees, at CWT, which had 22,000 employees, and at Best Buy with its 125,000 employees. The overall size of the company did not make any difference in my approach. Management should not be viewed as leading masses.

During one employee focus group, a young Blue Shirt pointed out what a difference being seen as an individual made to him. He had been hired at 18 years old, shy and unsure of himself. When asked about meaningful experiences at Best Buy, he immediately remembered his district manager's visit to his store. The district manager, who had met him when he was hired, recognized him and knew his name. This one small connection left a lasting impression. He wasn't just a Blue Shirt. He was an individual who was known and who mattered. Two years in, the once shy, unsure kid was blossoming and confident.

When I think back over my dreaded summer job in a grocery store as a teenager (chapter 1), I realize now that no one there knew who I was. I felt like I did not matter, and neither did my actions. As CEO of

Best Buy, I did my best to make all employees feel that both they and their job were important.

In *Hidden Value,* Stanford professors Charles O'Reilly and Jeffrey Pfeffer look at companies that are extraordinarily successful not because they have better or smarter people, but because they've figured out how to get the best out of their people and help all stakeholders thrive.[2] So-called "firms of endearment" recognize the value that each person can contribute, regardless of rank.[3] They treat employees the way customers should be treated—with respect and a deep understanding of their needs.

Respect starts with acknowledgment and recognition. French philosopher René Descartes famously said *Cogito ergo sum*—"I think, therefore I am." When it comes to creating a truly human organization, I believe there is a more powerful declaration: *Ego videor ergo sum*—"I am seen, therefore I am." In Ralph Ellison's classic 1952 novel, *Invisible Man,* the main character, an African American man, recounts the many ways in which he experiences social invisibility. I was struck by how poignantly relevant it still is today. In 2016, Best Buy organized focus groups of minority employees and managers. Although most Hispanic and Asian employees were generally doing fine, our Black and African American colleagues did not feel valued or even seen (more on this later in this chapter).

Respect means embracing people for who they are and as they are. After a transgender employee came to the HR team to explain that Best Buy did not cover her fully through her transition journey, the company looked at existing benefits and decided to cover aesthetic procedures such as pectoral implants and facial feminization. Kamy Scarlett, the head of HR, summed up perfectly why we'd made the change when only one employee came forward: "Because she is enough."

Creating a Safe and Transparent Environment to Foster Trust

On Black Friday 2014, my phone buzzed at 4 a.m. It was Mary Lou Kelley, Best Buy's head of e-commerce, calling to say that our website was down because of the traffic surge. On the busiest, most important day of the year, this was potentially devastating. There was only one thing to do: pull together and fix it. We did. That holiday season, comparable sales rose for the first time in four years.

When I think about trust, I often think about that phone call. Bad news has to travel at least as fast as good news, and that requires trusting that whatever problem arises, everyone will focus on fixing it, not doling out blame. Trust grows out of supporting each other, particularly during difficult times. Had Mary Lou feared that she might get fired for admitting what was happening, I might not have received that call.

Genuine human connections only flourish when people trust one another. In *Conscious Capitalism*, John Mackey, the co-CEO of Whole Foods, and Raj Sisodia define trust and caring as two key elements of what they label "conscious culture."[4] Without trust there is fear. And fear kills engagement and creativity. Building trust requires four things. First, it takes time. Second, it requires that you do what you say you are going to do. Third, you must be approachable: you cannot trust whom you cannot see. And fourth, you must be transparent.

Kamy and so many other Best Buy employees feel safe sharing their stories, and their openness encourages others to be vulnerable as well.[5] Safety is a basic human need. Safety was the foundation of former Ford CEO Alan Mulally's green-amber-red system, which encouraged executives to flag problems and their colleagues to help solve them. When making mistakes or not knowing or just being imperfectly human are seen as weaknesses, no one feels safe.

Alan Mulally is a master at fostering trust and safety by establishing and enforcing a clear behavior code. At Ford, everybody was expected never to use humor at the expense of someone else or criticize someone not in the room. Everyone was expected to fully support the team. The members of Alan's team needed to feel that they could trust each other to be supportive. Alan had zero tolerance for behaviors that deviated from these rules. He was famous for interrupting his weekly Business Plan Review meetings if he caught people checking their phones or engaging in any side discussion. He would stare down the culprits. "Let us all help you," he would say, "since you are doing something that is obviously more important than saving the Ford Motor company." It was a matter of respect, which built trust, and of keeping everyone focused. "That's okay," he would eventually say with a smile to anyone who did not live up to the expected behaviors. "You do not need to work here. It's up to you."

Encouraging Vulnerability

"Vulnerability is the glue that binds relationships together," says Brené Brown, who has written several books on the topic.[6] By being vulnerable and showing up as who we truly are, she explains, we're able to find compassion, genuine belonging, and authentic connection. And that authenticity, she concludes, is the birthplace of creativity, joy, and love.[7] The way to create more love and care at work, besides hiring and promoting people who are loving and caring, is to allow love and care to be more openly expressed.[8]

Having company leaders such as Kamy share her struggle with depression signals that we all share a human journey, and people should not hide who they are or be shy to ask for help. CEOs must participate too. When I arrived at Best Buy, I shared with my team that this turnaround was going to be hard and required that each of us be the best leader we could be, starting with me. I told my team that my executive coach, Marshall Goldsmith, was going to gather some feedback from each of them on how I was doing. After receiving feedback, I thanked my team and shared with them what three things I had picked to try to get better at. I think it helped set the tone for the turnaround.

Yet allowing myself to be vulnerable has not come easily to me. Although I am now able to embrace imperfection and feedback, I was brought up believing that professional and personal lives are kept separate and that emotions have little place at work. I am also rather private by nature. When I joined Best Buy, I threw myself into the turnaround and parked the pain of my recent divorce, which had left me saddled with a sense of failure. It took me several years to open up about it to friends, which helped me not only process these feelings and heal, but also show up at work as my whole self. This in turn enabled me to lead with my heart and my gut, and not just my head.

Being vulnerable isn't the same as sharing everything about one's personal life, however: the point is to share something authentic, relevant, and helpful to others.[9] So when, at the Holiday Leadership Meeting in 2019, one employee shared how she grew up with alcoholic parents, did not study past high school, and had been in a same-sex relationship, it wasn't just a "get-to-know-me" story. The visibly moved employee said these were all things that she had been ashamed of and never thought she would share. But she was sharing her story because it *was* relevant in the context of the meeting: she had found a home and a safe place at work, which gave her the courage and the space to be herself, trust again, and find forgiveness. She was being vulnerable to encourage and inspire others to be themselves as well and to find their own voice.

Vulnerability like that takes courage. But like this leader and Kamy's story have demonstrated, when you are being vulnerable in environments where trust has been established and respect is a given, people want to help you. And you are also giving them license to ask for help. This is what builds places in which people support each other and why such companies are often described, like Best Buy often is, as a family.

Leadership requires combining vulnerability with making sometimes tough decisions and giving hope. Marriott CEO Arne Sorenson's video message to employees on March 19, 2020, in the midst of the Covid-19 pandemic, is a master class in emotional intelligence and vulnerability. He appeared, shockingly to many, without his full head of hair, because of treatment for pancreatic cancer. He first talked about employees directly affected by the virus, offering support. He then explained that the impact of the pandemic and the restrictions taken to contain the outbreak were battering Marriott's hospitality business.

There was no sugarcoating, but no panic either as he went on to explain what the company was doing to mitigate the crisis. New hires were paused, and costs such as marketing and advertising cut. He would not take any salary for the rest of the year, and his executive team would take a 50 percent pay cut. Work weeks were being shortened around the world, and temporary leave was implemented.

He then focused on signs of recovery in China, which offered hope to the rest of the world. "I can tell you that I've never had a more difficult moment than this one," he said, reflecting on his eight years as CEO of Marriott. "There is simply nothing worse than telling highly valued associates, people who are the very heart of this company, that their roles are being impacted by events completely outside of their control," he added, his voice breaking. "I've never been more determined to see us through than I am at this moment."

He concluded on a hopeful note, projecting to the day when the global community would come through to the other side of the pandemic, and people would start traveling again. "When that great day comes, we will be there to welcome them, with the warmth and care we are known for the world over." His message was honest, heartfelt, and moving, while at the same time uplifting and inspiring.[10]

Developing Effective Team Dynamics

To create high-performing teams, the best version of every individual must translate into the best version of the collective. And this requires leveraging human connections.

In 2016, Best Buy was transitioning from its Renew Blue turnaround to its growth strategy, and it was time to shift gears from making sure we had the right individuals in the right jobs to getting our teams to perform better. We called in executive coach Eric Pliner to work with senior executives, including myself (chapter 3). Initially, the goal was to improve the performance of each of us, but it shifted quickly because, as Eric says, "the best teams are A teams, not collections of A players."

We had A players, but we did not yet have an A team.

Eric diagnosed two reasons why. First, the executives tended to have hero mentalities: they were high performers who sought to fix problems, as individuals. Second, caretaking was valued over caring. This is a subtle but crucial distinction. People were kind to a fault, so they avoided delivering hard messages rather than risk hurting a colleague's feelings.

So first, Eric established where each of us stood on a number of dimensions, such as the need for interaction or control or reflection, or likelihood of becoming emotional, to help us understand how we differed from each other. Then he gave us feedback individually and mapped each of us on a chart. Finally, to make it really stick, he got us to stand in different places around the room so that we could experience physically where we were positioned relative to each other on each of these dimensions. Not only was it fun to see where everyone was "plotted," but it also gave a visual, and then physical, sense of how similar and different we were.

Understanding each other's different needs and wiring when interacting with others equipped us to better relate to one another. This did not mean any of us needed to change, but it became much easier to see how we each could irritate someone else and understand the consequences of our own behavior. Live in that room, we moved from "I find it irritating when you do this" to "If I present this differently, we can both get what we need."

Another telling moment was when Eric asked these senior executives who their primary team was. They all said their primary team was their functional team—whether merchandising, marketing, supply chain, retail, finance, or HR. No one said the executive team—the team doing the exercise—was his or her team. We were still a collection of players. This started changing when Mike Mohan, who was then the chief merchant, affirmed that he needed to make the executive team his primary team.

To strengthen our connections, we also learned to move from caretaking to caring. "I do not want to hurt your feelings" would give way to candid feedback. We practiced with a "continue-start-stop" exercise, telling each other what we should continue doing, start doing, and stop doing when relating to one another. We moved from being "Minnesota nice" to far more open and honest.

Over several years, we invested one day every quarter—about a work week per year—working with Eric on becoming a more effective executive team. If you had told me 20 or even 10 years ago that I would be investing that kind of time in something like building better relationships at work, I would have shaken my head in disbelief. Really? We are going to spend a day or a day and a half talking about ourselves, our feelings, and how we relate to each other? The previous version of me didn't yet understand how much more valuable it was to invest a week in becoming a more effective team than to spend that time poring over spreadsheets or sales figures.

Promoting Diversity and Inclusion

Unleashing human magic by celebrating employees as individuals is, at its very core, about diversity and inclusion. As I write this in 2020, it has become even more obvious that diversity and inclusion are existential issues that must be addressed. Fostering environments that promote diversity greatly improves employee engagement and company performance.[11] Seen in this light, diversity and inclusion are not a sideshow. They are key business imperatives.

When I talk about diversity and inclusion in the context of creating human magic, I mean creating space for every individual to contribute and be valued for who they are, as they are, with their unique perspective and experience. This of course covers gender, race, ethnicity, and sexual orientation. I also include considerations such as cognitive, age, social, and cultural diversity.

Although many companies are committed to becoming more diverse, change has been too slow. We are wired to favor people who look like us and think like us, which perpetuates systemic exclusion, particularly when it comes to gender and race. It takes more than good intentions or a diversity, equity, and inclusion program to tackle existing imbalances. It takes bold and sustained actions. It takes leadership. And it was during my years at Best Buy that I learned the most about diversity and inclusion.

Back in 2012, Best Buy was fairly diverse and representative when it came to its Blue Shirts. But from the store manager level up, everyone became progressively whiter and more male. Women made up fewer than one in five store managers, for instance, and all territory managers were men. The field had traditionally been an old boys' network, which felt uncomfortable for many women. Few managerial positions were held by people of color, particularly African Americans. The racial imbalance partly reflected local demographics: historically, Minnesota

had been on the paler side of the racial spectrum, populated by immigrants from Germany, Scandinavia, Finland, and Ireland. Yet more recently, the state has become more diverse, now home to a growing
community of Latino, Somali, and Asian immigrants. That diversity
was not reflected at Best Buy beyond the store floors.

We had work to do.

We started at the top. If employees cannot see someone who looks
like them among their managers and in the boardroom, they don't
feel they have a shot. And if they feel they have few prospects, they
cannot be fully engaged and give their best. I was fortunate to be able
to quickly redress imbalances in the executive team. There is ample
research confirming that companies with more women in their top
management perform better.[12] My long experience working with
women had confirmed as much: Marilyn Carlson Nelson had been my
boss throughout my years first at Carlson Wagonlit Travel and then at
Carlson; when I was in charge of Vivendi Games, I also reported to a
woman, Agnès Touraine.

Formidable women soon held key positions on Best Buy's executive
team, from CFO Sharon McCollam and head of stores Shari Ballard
to Mary Lou Kelley, in charge of e-commerce, which led *Fortune* magazine to run an article headlined "Meet the Women Who Saved Best
Buy" in 2015.[13] From experience and study, I had gained insight that
helped ensure that women would get noticed and promoted as they
deserved. Women's leadership expert Sally Helgesen and my former
coach, Marshall Goldsmith, for example, highlighted in their book 12
habits that often stand in the way of successful women becoming more
successful—quirks that are different from those that men tend to ex-
hibit.[14] Women, for example, typically find it more difficult than men
to claim achievements or put themselves forward for a job unless they
meet every single requirement or more. I distributed Sally and Marshall's book to all leaders at Best Buy. I wanted everyone to understand we had to put our thumb on the scale to account for differences

in behavior. Otherwise, nothing ever changes. In the first half of its fiscal year 2019, 58 percent of Best Buy's external hires at the corporate level were women. And in 2019, Best Buy named its first woman CEO, Corie Barry.

Revisiting Best Buy's board of directors was also part of diversity efforts. We needed more diverse skills, perspectives, and experience than we had on our board, to support a major turnaround and then a major growth campaign. Starting in 2013, we recruited individuals who had experience in successfully transforming large enterprises; directors who had a strong focus on innovation, technology, data, and e-commerce; and more recently leaders with experience in the health sector. As I write these lines in 2020, Best Buy's directors now represent a diverse mix of skills, gender, and ethnicities—all of whom have made invaluable contributions. Out of 13 board members, three directors are African American and seven are women. Effective diversity at the board level is about finding the right skills and building critical mass—not tokenism—so different perspectives and views achieve better outcomes.[15]

Racial imbalances among employees turned out to be more challenging to redress. In 2016, focus groups I ran with minority employees and managers made one thing painfully clear to me: our African American colleagues often felt stuck at entry-level positions, with few prospects for advancement. At headquarters, they felt trapped in the call center, hardly ever considered for promotions. Best Buy's General Counsel Keith Nelsen, as executive sponsor of the Black Employee Resource Group, was batting hard on behalf of Black candidates, but they never got the jobs. Many employees of color were from other parts of the country and felt displaced in Minnesota. They found little awareness or understanding among their local colleagues that their life experiences were different from your average Minnesotan's.

I was blown away, and frankly hurt, by what I heard in these focus groups. As a white Frenchman living in Minnesota, I had had very limited exposure to the challenges that people of color face. I was also aware that my experience in driving real change when it came to diversity of all kinds was limited. I needed to do more, starting with better understanding the depth of systemic obstacles facing minorities, especially our African American colleagues.

One of the initiatives introduced by Howard Rankin, who drove our diversity and inclusion efforts, was a "reverse" mentor program that paired Best Buy executives with employees who would mentor them to help broaden their understanding of differences. I was incredibly lucky to have Laura Gladney, an African American mother of two working in supply chain management at Best Buy, as my mentor. Our monthly discussions helped me see the world in general, and Best Buy in particular, through her eyes, which helped me measure the weight of history and what it means to be African American in the United States today. I learned how, for example, the once vibrant Rondo community in St. Paul, Minnesota, was eviscerated in the late 1950s and 1960s when the I-94 freeway was built right through its neighborhood, displacing families and killing local businesses. On a more personal level, Laura echoed the view expressed by many of her colleagues about the lack of career development opportunities, which had almost led her to leave the company. She also helped me gain a deeper understanding of Historically Black Colleges and Universities, which made me realize we were missing out on recruitment grounds rich in talent.

At the suggestion of colleagues, I also met Mellody Hobson, the president and co-CEO of Chicago financial management company Ariel Investments, and a director in a number of boards, including Starbucks's and JP Morgan's. "You need to put it in business terms," she told me over coffee in New York. Companies must reflect the demographics of their customers to be able to understand and address their needs. She explained how, for example, many hands-free faucets and soap dispensers in public bathrooms were a source of frustration for African Americans because the infrared technology did not work well with dark skin. In companies full of white employees, no one had thought of testing the technology on darker skins. There is no shortage of similar examples, including Google Photos' infamous tagging and widespread biases in facial recognition software because of insufficient diversity in the racial makeup of development teams and photo databases.[16]

Best Buy's drive toward better diversity and inclusion has centered on workforce, workplace, suppliers, and community. We expanded our recruitment efforts by widening our slate of job candidates. This has included establishing a recruitment program and scholarships with Historically Black Colleges and Universities. In the first half of its fiscal year 2019, people of color made up 20 percent of Best Buy's external hires at the corporate level and 50 percent of external recruits in stores.

Yet change is slow. Best Buy typically prefers internal hires, which, while offering many advantages, slows progress on diversity. In addition, turnover remains higher among employees of color, even though the gap has narrowed. There is more work to be done.

Besides pushing for more diverse recruitment, we worked hard to better support minority employees. A one-on-one diversity mentorship program was set up to help advance careers. Diversity and inclusion are now part of how all Best Buy's officers are evaluated.

Best Buy, like other companies, is also leveraging its buying power to influence suppliers. For example, I encouraged our general counsel to explain to law firms that we expected the teams assigned to work with us to be diverse; otherwise, we would be happy to work with someone else.

Such a push toward diversity invariably leads to some discomfort. Making more space for underrepresented groups is often seen as squeezing other people out. When, in 2016, I mentioned during an address to Best Buy employees that the face of the company, like much of corporate America's, was still largely "pale, male, and stale," one employee felt insulted and complained to our human resources department. My words were meant to be self-deprecating—there is no denying that I am, after all, a white man myself—but I apologized.

The way I see it, this gives white males like myself an excellent opportunity to realize how privileged we have been and to feel what so many others have felt in the past. At the same time, the zero-sum-game perspective misses the point that, without diversity, everyone eventually suffers. Just take a look at Lehman Brothers. If it had been Lehman Brothers & Sisters, I am convinced the story would have been very different.

. . .

Best Buy has received multiple accolades for being a great place to work for all by the likes of Forbes and Glassdoor. When asked about what makes it so, most employees repeat similar themes: it's like a family; it feels like home. This is part of why they want to go to work in the morning. That sense of connection stems from respect, trust, vulnerability, and effective team dynamics, as well as diversity and inclusion.

Such strong human connections within the company, added to a sense of purpose, contribute to creating the kind of human magic that creates irrational performance.

Next is the third of our five human-magic ingredients: autonomy.

Questions to Reflect On

- Do you have friends at work?

- Do you feel that you are seen as a unique individual at work? What do you do to give others that sense?

- Do you feel you can trust your team? Why or why not?

- How comfortable are you being vulnerable at work? How comfortable are you when others are vulnerable? Why or why not?

- Do you relate to different team members in different ways, based on their communication style and preferences?

- How do you promote diversity and inclusion at work? What else could you do?

11

Third Ingredient: Fostering Autonomy

Human beings have an innate inner drive to be autonomous, self-determined, and connected to one another. And when that drive is liberated, people achieve more and live richer lives.

—Daniel Pink, *Drive: The Surprising Truth about What Motivates Us*

When I met Maurice Grange in 1986, he had been in charge of maintenance at computer company Honeywell Bull in Paris for many years. I was a young McKinsey consultant, part of a team helping the company improve its customer service. I was struck by how widely customer satisfaction ratings varied from one district to another, but once aggregated at the regional level, produced more even results as districts balanced each other out.

During a meeting, I argued that Maurice Grange should be looking at the district level to better understand what was driving performance and hold his regional managers accountable for district results. "Young man," Maurice said, "let me tell you about the theory of the mare."

The theory of the mare? I had no idea what he was talking about. But I was curious.

Think of a mare on a farm, he said. The mare limps and is visibly in pain. She has a stone stuck in her hoof. A vet is called. The vet has to lift her hoof to extract the stone with a hook. But if the vet holds the hoof, the mare needs support to stand and will gradually put more and more weight on the vet. There is no way the vet could carry the horse's full weight without getting crushed. The only solution is for the vet to let go, as this will force the mare to stand up on her own.

Maurice Grange was saying that, if as a manager you try to carry your team and fix their problems, they will lean on you more and more. It may be tempting in the short term, but you keep shouldering more weight, which will crush you. If Maurice got involved at the district level, he would be doing the regional managers' job on their behalf. Instead, he had to let them stand on their own feet.

This was a long way from the scientific management and strategic planning approach I had been schooled in, which former secretary of defense Robert McNamara exemplified. The approach was to plan, organize, direct, and control, based on the idea that management could be a pure science. A small team of smart people at the top, informed by data and statistical analysis, decided on a rational plan, which then trickled down. McNamara's years at the Pentagon came to be defined by the United States' disastrous involvement in Vietnam. As he himself later came to realize, analysis obsessively based on quantifiable data alone leaves out crucial human intangibles like motivation and hope or disengagement and resentment. It is also vulnerable to bias and flawed data. Humans—and therefore leaders—are not all-knowing and infallible.[1]

Decades later, however, McNamara's analytical, top-down approach was still dominant in business. After listening to Maurice Grange's mare theory, my first instinct was to push back. My love of data and deductive reasoning blinded me to the reality that, while of course very useful, they do not have to lead to a command and control approach that is no longer in sync with today's environment. In our new reality, being nimble and innovative is crucial. The need for emotional intelligence, speed, and flexibility means that employee autonomy—letting them carry their own weight—has become essential to success.

In most cases, decisions cannot—and should not—trickle down from the top.

You may ask: What does this have to do with human magic? Autonomy, or the ability to control what you do, when you do it, and with whom, is one of the fundamental elements of what intrinsically motivates us, which leads directly to better performance.[2] Autonomy leads us to think creatively, which breeds innovation. Innovation does not happen without the freedom to try out new ideas. Autonomy is also motivating because it is more satisfying. Few people enjoy being told what to do. I know I do not. And research has shown that stress levels at work are directly related not only to how demanding a job is, but also to the latitude one has to control and organize one's own work.[3] The less freedom, the more draining work gets.

You create an environment where autonomy helps generate human magic (and not the chaos of everyone doing whatever they want) by:

- Pushing decision making as far down as possible

- Preferring a participative process

- Adopting agile ways of working

- Adjusting to skill and will

Let us take them one by one.

Let It Go! Pushing Decision Making
as Far Down as Possible

In 2016, Corie Barry and I were on a flight to San Antonio. Back then, Corie was in charge of our strategic growth office, coming up with and testing new ideas and initiatives as part of the just-announced Building the New Blue growth strategy. One idea that Corie's team was testing was in-home advisors. The team had designed a pilot that was running in San Antonio. Corie and I were going there so I could see the test in action.

During the flight, Corie gave me a presentation deck to read about the new initiative: the pilot program had shown excellent results, and an expansion to Florida and Atlanta markets would make sense as a next step. Keen to clarify the exact purpose of my visit, I asked Corie if I was going to San Antonio to decide whether to roll out to these new markets. "No!" she told me. "I have already made that decision!"

I broke into a huge grin. This was the kind of autonomy we needed—that all companies need—to thrive. The only reason I was going to San Antonio was to see our initiative firsthand and stay informed.

This reflected a shift that we, the executive team, had been working on with the help of coach Eric Pliner. To improve our effectiveness as a team (see chapter 10), he had us work on how we were making decisions. In the turnaround crisis mode, I had been in the driver's seat when it came to important decisions. It was time to change that.

The first thing we looked at was *who* should be making decisions, meaning at what level in the organization decisions should be made. He argued that decisions should be made at the lowest possible echelon within the organization, which is the place where people have either enough or the best information to make that decision. The lowest possible place is rarely at the top. But in a large retailer like

Best Buy, this push down isn't trivial. The company is really a single-business business, organized by function such as merchandising, marketing, and channels, which tends to push decisions all the way up to where these functions meet.

Nonetheless, we had opportunities. For example, store managers used to rely on a centrally developed sales script to train Blue Shirts and guide their conversations with customers. It quickly became obvious that if sales associates were to authentically connect with customers, they had to be given the latitude to be themselves and make decisions on their own. Once our purpose of enhancing the lives of customers through technology had become clear, what our associates needed was the autonomy to do just that in a way that felt true to each one of them. What cascaded down was the "why" of intent and purpose. Not the "how to" of a rigid sales script. This could only work in the environment of trust and respect outlined in chapter 10.

Amazon's "disagree and commit" ethos illustrates this approach to making decisions. In a letter to shareholders explaining why the company should always look at every day as Day One, Jeff Bezos recounts how he felt that the case for a proposed Amazon Studios original production was not convincing. But his team felt otherwise, so the program went ahead with his full backing. "Note what this example is not," he explains. "It's not me thinking to myself 'well, these guys are wrong and missing the point, but this isn't worth me chasing.' It's a genuine disagreement of opinion, a candid expression of my view, a chance for the team to weigh my view, and a quick, sincere commitment to go their way."[4]

In addition to *who* should be making decisions, Eric also had us work on *how* decisions should be made. With his help, we learned to leverage the framework known as RASCI, which stands for responsible, accountable, support, consult, and inform. We reviewed a number of decisions and discussed who should be assigned to each category with each decision.

Ultimately, I was left with a few decisions for which I was *account-able* and would provide *support*. I had a lot of decisions in which I'd be *consulted* or merely *informed*. In the end, I was personally *responsible* for basically four decisions: the overall strategy of the company; major investment decisions, especially mergers and acquisitions; who was on the executive team; and setting the tone for the values of the company. I would be consulted on a number of decisions, of course, and offer my views on things like branding and capital structure. But ultimately it was up to the head of marketing and the CFO to make those decisions. In many cases—like the in-home advisor rollout—I only needed to be informed. Besides introducing far more autonomy into the system, our new modus operandi also avoided the opposite pitfall of spinning our wheels into paralysis, with everybody voicing an opinion but no one making a decision.

We moved into a more decentralized mode. This was perfect for our growth strategy, but a notable change from our Renew Blue turn-around mode, during which I had made a lot of decisions to steady the Best Buy ship. Habits needed to be broken, and this was an adjustment. Improving the way we related to each other, described in chapter 10, greatly supported the shift. We trusted each other to make the best possible decisions, but were also ready to offer assistance and honest feedback whenever needed. When we started working with Eric, everyone on the team kept looking in my direction whenever a final word needed to be spoken on any topic. "Don't look at me!" I kept saying with a smile. Eventually, we transitioned to far more de-centralized decisions, which greatly clarified, accelerated, and im-proved how we operated.

This reminded me of my experience as president of EDS France. The CEO of Nike in the country had given me a batch of "Just Do It!" stickers. Whenever someone at EDS came up with an idea, I would give them one of these stickers. I wanted everyone to feel that they could run with their ideas and try them out. I also wanted them to know that they were allowed to make mistakes. If new ideas did not work out, they would learn and correct course.

Creating a Participative Process

While still a consultant at McKinsey, I worked in a small town in central France with a factory that made batteries for missile systems. The factory needed to improve its operational performance. We used a four-step improvement process spanning roughly eight weeks. First, a baseline was set along with targets for improvement. The targets had to be ambitious enough to avoid marginal tweaks in process and force a radical rethinking. Second, everyone was involved to generate ideas of how things could be improved. The best ideas, however, typically came from front liners, who directly experienced what process was clunky and often already knew what could work better. Third, ideas were sorted into three buckets: Yes (strong idea), No (too expensive and/or risky), and Maybe (potentially promising). Fourth, we'd set up next steps for the Yes and Maybe ideas.

Senior management's role was to mostly stay out of the way: they organized and ran the process that allowed the plant workers and their direct supervisors to come up with the ideas.

For a young McKinsey consultant still steeped in the command and control model, the results were mind-blowing. Plant workers came up with a wide range of concrete ideas that no one at headquarters could have ever imagined. Although these operational projects were not considered particularly glamorous within McKinsey, this turned out to be an enlightening experience—and a crucial lesson that I never forgot.

Inviting similar broad-based input may have come easier for me than others for a reason: throughout my career, I have been blessed to lead companies in sectors I knew nothing about when I arrived. In many ways, I had no choice but to trust and empower others. My outsider status was an effective antidote against any temptation I might have had to revert to a top-down approach to strategy. When I joined Carlson Wagonlit Travel, the company needed a growth plan to present at the next board meeting. This was my third CEO rodeo, after EDS France and Vivendi Games, and by then I knew that my job was not to come up with answers. Even if I'd wanted to, I couldn't have: my only experience with the business travel industry was to have traveled. My job was to create and drive a process that allowed those who knew the business far better than I did to find answers. At CWT, we effectively mimicked the four-step approach that I had learned at the battery-making factory: What is our situation today? Where do we want to go? What do we need to do to get there? How exactly are we going to do it? We organized offsite workshops with teams from all functions, from HR to marketing, to supply management, to IT. I did not come up with ideas and solutions. I asked questions, supported the team in the creation of a plan, helped synthesize it and presented it to the board.

When I later moved to Carlson, it was the same. The only experience I had with the hospitality industry was to have stayed at hotels and eaten at restaurants. So I orchestrated a process by which every business unit had to come up with a plan to grow.

You may recall that I had no retail experience when I joined Best Buy, and we had to come up with a turnaround plan in eight weeks. That plan, as described in chapter 7, was created through workshops with inputs from the team and validated with Best Buy's officers before being presented to the board and to investors. That little battery factory had no idea how influential it turned out to be.

There was one crucial difference at Best Buy, however: ideas and solutions came from every unit, but I made a lot of decisions myself initially, from matching online prices to reinstating the employee discount. Why? Because the house was burning. Once the company had safely stepped back from the brink and we'd devised our Building the

New Blue growth strategy in 2016, I adopted a far more hands-off approach to making decisions.

Adopting Agile Ways of Working

In 2018, Best Buy's chief digital and technology officer Brian Tilzer took the executive team on a trip to downtown Minneapolis. Our destination was the headquarters of US Bank. Brian wanted us to better understand a new way of working by seeing it in action. Following the 2008 Great Recession, the bank—like all other major banks in the United States—had had to adopt much stricter risk management and compliance across its operations. This had naturally contributed to a more rigid and less innovative environment. My friend Tim Welsh, who had recently become vice-chairman of consumer and business banking there, was now leading an effort to make the bank more customer friendly. Instead of having siloed departments and decisions trickle down the corporate food chain, US Bank created teams of people representing multiple functions, from technology and HR to marketing, legal, and finance, and these teams called the shots. This is how, for example, US Bank found ways to approve small business loans or mortgages much faster, in spite of the heavier compliance requirements imposed after the recession.

In short, US Bank had become agile.

Many companies are adopting small, autonomous multifunctional teams working in sprints to vastly accelerate decisions and adjustments. Our visit showed us enough to convince the Best Buy executive team to give the new approach a go. We first applied it to e-commerce. We quickly were able to move from upgrading the website a few times per year to making changes several times a week, based on data (not on what the CEO thought) and ongoing, real-time testing.

We then rolled out the agile approach across multiple projects and processes, including pricing and promotions as well as employee facing tools. This is probably one of the things that, during the Covid-19 crisis in March 2020, helped Best Buy move its operations to contactless curbside pickup in only three days, something that could have otherwise taken at least three quarters.

Adjusting to Skill and Will

Delegating decisions and fostering autonomy, though crucial, are not appropriate in all situations.

When I started at Best Buy in 2012, the parking lot at our Richfield headquarters looked surprisingly empty. I found out that on any given day, between a fifth and a third of people employed at our headquarters were not at the office. In some departments, team meetings were half empty. Best Buy's corporate employees were allowed to work from wherever they wanted, whenever they wanted, as long as they delivered expected results. This was known as ROWE—results only work environment.

In February 2013, still early in our turnaround, our executive team fiercely debated whether we should continue with this program. Our CFO Sharon McCollam was dead set against the system, which she believed lowered productivity. Others did not think it was material enough for us to focus on. I had to intervene and break the deadlock.

In the end, I decided to scrap remote working, which, as you might suspect, was not a unanimously popular decision. Some people, including those who designed the system, thought I was a management dinosaur, more interested in having people clock in than in results. I received e-mails that cited scenarios involving sick children and elderly parents—when no one had ever suggested there would be no sick leave or exception. As a coincidence, Yahoo's CEO, Marissa Mayer, had just scrapped the company's own version of remote working.

In today's world, after Covid-19 made remote working necessary, including at Best Buy, this choice seems outdated. But back then, without the public health considerations that have now made remote work a necessity, I reached that decision for practical and philosophical reasons.

From a practical standpoint, Best Buy was on the brink of death. It was an emergency situation, which meant that we had to work together, act fast, stay synced, and keep information flowing. All that required having people in the same place at the same time. A patient dying on the table is best served by a medical team all in the room. In addition, remote working did not apply to everyone. Having different rules for different parts of the company was breeding tension and resentment. Store employees did not have the option to work from home: they had to pitch up, and they had to pitch up on time.

Second, the program was built on the idea that delegation is always the right approach, an idea that I thought was fundamentally flawed. There is no one-size-fits-all leadership approach that works in all situations and for all individuals. I had learned, when I attended my first management training at McKinsey in the mid-1980s, that autonomy must be calibrated to skills and motivation—specific contexts demand specific tactics.[5]

Delegation only works with people who have sufficient ability and motivation. If you ask me to build a brick wall or cook a five-course dinner and let me get on with it, the results are going to be very disappointing. And if I were a mason with experience but no interest in building a wall, results would be equally terrible.

Delegation and autonomy lead to human magic only when people are *both* skilled and motivated. When I had that summer job at a garage as a teenager, I was neither motivated nor skilled (chapter 1). Autonomy would not have helped me—or the garage.

Blizzard Entertainment was a textbook example of a high-skill, high-will combination. The video game studio that was part of Vivendi Games when I was CEO was a leader in its field. Its developers were brilliant and avid gamers themselves. I would not have dreamed of dictating what the new games should be or when they should be launched: Blizzard was in charge. The company knew best when games were ready.

That expertise did not extend to marketing and distribution, however. The success of the company's *Starcraft* game in the United States, for example, was not matched when *Starcraft* was later released in Europe and Asia, because games were getting pirated as soon as they had been released in North America. As a result, the large European retailers did not invest in the distribution of the product. The studio was frustrated with the international sales team, and the international sales team was none too pleased with the studio. To solve the problem, I organized a workshop in London that brought the two teams together. The goal was to develop a good diagnosis and have the combined team come up with concrete solutions together.

The workshop led to the implementation of copy protection on games and a commitment to orchestrate a global, simultaneous launch of Blizzard's next blockbuster video game, *Diablo II*. Combined, these two decisions would limit piracy and increase buzz for the sales teams. The game ended up being a huge success, prompting the *New York Times* to draw parallels with the success of the Harry Potter book series.[6] I had chosen to lead within the context: in this case, where passions were high but problem-solving skills weren't, it had been appropriate to choose intervention over autonomy by creating a forum where the issue at hand could be solved.

Likewise, at Best Buy, in the 2012 context of saving the company, the right approach was to be directive. Although a lot of people contributed to devising our turnaround plan, I started off by making many of the decisions. In the 2016 context of a stable company intent on growth, we needed big ideas and innovation, and we were ready for more autonomy and trying new things. I launched a system of "get-out-of-jail-free" cards (we produced physical cards) to be used when initiatives flamed out. This gave people a chance to innovate while taking off the pressure to always succeed.

. . .

A company purpose aligned with individual drive, authentic human connections, and autonomy all influence how much of ourselves we are ready to invest at work. But human magic also requires that we get opportunities to become great at what we do best. That's next: mastery.

Questions to Reflect On

- How does autonomy influence your own engagement?

- How is strategy determined in the organization or team you lead?

- How do you involve others in the process?

- What decisions do you own? How are you making these decisions?

- How much autonomy do you grant your team? How does it manifest?

- Do you adjust your leadership style according to the situation? If so, how? What criteria do you use? How do you adjust?

12

Fourth Ingredient: Achieving Mastery

The streak was never our goal.

—Bob Ladouceur, coach of the Spartans, the De La Salle High School football team in California

The De La Salle Spartans of Concord, California, seemed to have mastered high school football: the team was undefeated for 151 games—the longest streak in football history at any level, by a long shot. One hundred and fifty-one games! This is human magic producing irrational performance.

De La Salle's players were not the biggest; the team was not the most well-heeled. They did not outspend or out recruit other towns to achieve this amazing streak. They just followed an extraordinary leader and coach, Bob Ladouceur, who, besides giving the players an unshakable sense of purpose and team spirit, drove them to strive to be the best possible version of themselves. "Nobody on this staff expects you to play perfect tonight. It's impossible," Coach Ladouceur would tell his team before a game. "But what we do expect, and what you should expect from yourself and each other, is a perfect effort."

Coach Ladouceur trained his team to strive for mastery—becoming skilled through instruction and practice in something that gives you joy. Jean-Marie Descarpentries, who shared with me his People → Business → Finance approach to business, also liked to say that in his view, the ultimate goal of a company just may be the growth and fulfillment of everyone working there.

At a minimum, employees' growth and fulfillment are essential to performance, and the role of leaders is to create the environment that allows for mastery—like De La Salle's coach did. Ironically, a sustained focus on mastery and process, rather than on outcomes themselves, is what consistently delivers the best possible results. Mastery is essential to performance because becoming great at what one does best is fundamentally satisfying and motivates us as human beings. Aikido enthusiast and teacher George Leonard argues that "the long-term, essentially goalless process of mastery" is a sure route to success and fulfillment in life.[1] People writing entries on Wikipedia, or the developers behind Linux and Apache, develop these resources during their free time for the world to use, in part because they enjoy applying their skills.

Mastery also supports the other ingredients of human magic: skilled people are of course more likely to perform better and, provided they are also motivated, can be given more autonomy.

"I appreciate efforts," one of my bosses at EDS once told me. "But I really care about performance." That's a tempting way to lead. It is easy to focus on performance gaps and just say "do better," but it probably won't work.

Creating an environment where mastery develops requires:

- Focusing on effort over results

- Developing individuals rather than the masses

- Coaching rather than training

- Reassessing performance assessment and development

- Treating learning as a lifelong journey

- Making space for failure

Focusing on Effort over Results

The fulfillment that mastery delivers lies in Bob Ladouceur's "best effort" rather than in the game results. It lies in the consistent practice for the sake of practice, rather than the outcome. (Masters love to practice.) So when the Spartan players lost game 152, ending their streak, they could still show up and give their all because they were still aiming for mastery and still loved doing it despite the streak being over. That focus allowed them to rebound and remain an outstanding team because their purpose was never about the streak.

In his book about the team, Neil Hayes reflects that "De La Salle separates itself from the competition because everyone from the head coach to the least accomplished player on the roster is willing to make the sacrifices necessary to be their absolute best."[2]

Skeptics might question how this translates to the business world. Mastery is a nice thought, but surely it must be subservient to outcome, right? No. Treating profits as a purpose in business undermines the mastery mindset by focusing on results over seeking fulfillment and best efforts as their own end. While visiting India, I spent time studying how Indian spirituality considers work. I was struck by how our criticism of profit as the main purpose of a corporation (chapter 4) echoes verse 2.47 of the *Gita*, the Hindu scripture. The verse suggests that obsessing about outcome makes us less effective— undermining the very outcome we are so invested in—and leads to frustration and resentment when results, which our actions determine only in part, fail to meet our expectations.[3]

Letting go of outcome is not easy. Focusing on result is natural for those of us who are competitive. But during my eight years at Best Buy, I realized that focusing on process—creating the best possible environment—is indeed what delivers the best outcome. It is like playing tennis: if you obsess about winning the point or the game, you are more likely to miss because you get tense. Your best game typically happens when you relax and focus on the ball.

Loving the process and striving to do our best keeps us motivated and ever more skilled over the long haul, which leads to irrational and lasting performance.

Developing the Individual, Not the Masses

In 2014, at the height of the Renew Blue turnaround, I visited Best Buy's operations in Denver, because something special was happening there. Over the course of a year, the average revenue per hour for each sales associate in the region had improved by $14 an hour, a 10 percent increase, unmatched anywhere else and without more customer traffic than other regions. If we could replicate this improvement across all stores, it would translate into $4–5 *billion* in added revenue.

Regional manager Chris Schmidt was the magician behind Denver's astonishing results. Chris thought that the top-down approach to sales management did not make sense. Everyone was asked to focus on the same things and approach customers in the same way, regardless of their individual abilities. Sales data for each associate was available, but most stores hardly used it. Chris had realized that mining that data could tell him where each person could improve. He focused on two metrics: revenue per hour and revenue mix. If one individual was lagging in revenue per hour, he or she might need tips on how to talk to customers or become more knowledgeable about the products and services available to better advise customers. Associates with top revenue per hour, on the other hand, did not need to focus on conversion, but could perhaps expand the suite of products or solutions that they sold.

Until then, Best Buy had always looked at improving productivity and performance in aggregate—by district or region—rather than at the level of individuals. Chris felt that was ineffective. Instead, he focused on mastery for every single individual, one person at a time. Luckily for Best Buy, he decided by himself to adopt that approach in his region. By the time I visited, Blue Shirts in Denver met one-on-one with their manager once a week. Together, they reviewed the previous week, decided where to target improvement for the coming week, and set a goal. They also identified career opportunities they could pursue over the longer term.

The sales associates were fired up. They loved being able to see exactly how they each contributed to their store, the district, and the company, and how that improved over time. They loved the highly personalized learning.

I was floored. Chris had furthered the overarching People → Business → Finance management philosophy I espoused and revolutionized how we would think about skills, performance, and mastery. We rolled out his approach nationwide, and it caught on like wildfire. Every month, there was a call with the top performers across the country so they could share their best practices. The new approach lifted skills and amplified motivation. It was one of the most critical changes we adopted during the turnaround.

Coaching Rather Than Training

In the late 1980s, I was part of a McKinsey team assisting Honeywell Bull's sales force to improve. The company used typical training programs that were by and large useless. Within a month of sitting in a classroom or listening to a presentation, most people forget a staggering 80 percent of what they were taught, unless the ideas are practiced on the job. The company's sales force—like everyone else—would learn better by doing and by repeating that doing in a practical context.

This is exactly what coaching does: it works on practical skills in real-life situations. Recognizing that traditional training was not helping, we assisted Honeywell Bull to pivot toward action learning and coaching. Sales teams attended workshops to learn new concepts and immediately work together on a real case they had brought to the program. District managers had been trained first, so they could coach their sales team during the workshop and then back on the job. Honeywell Bull saw tangible improvements in sales and margin.

I remembered this experience when I saw Chris's innovative approach to individualized feedback in Denver. During my visit, I was paired with one of the managers to experience the kind of weekly one-on-one meeting that fired up the sales associates there. I played the role of a Blue Shirt in the appliance department. My "manager" Jordan and I first reviewed my "results" on sales volume and revenue mix. It turned out that my revenue per hour was on the low side. My sales data showed that I sold fewer units per transaction than average. Jordan and I decided we would focus on this. I may have needed coaching in other areas, but Jordan knew that it's hard to learn multiple things at the same time. So we focused on this one metric and how to improve it.

We used roleplay so I could learn how to approach conversations with customers differently. Jordan became a sales associate, and I was a client coming to the store to replace a broken washing machine. After determining which machine would best fit my needs, Jordan asked how long I had had my washing machine.

"About 12 years," I said.

"Did you buy your dryer at the same time?" she asked.

"Yes," I ventured.

"How important is it to you to have a dryer that matches your washing machine?"

"Well, I like my laundry room to look tidy," I answered.

"Okay. The thing is, 12 years is a pretty good run for appliances of this kind. Chances are your dryer will die as well within the next year or two. Models tend to change every year, so you might not find a match to your washing machine in a year or two. We are currently offering promotions on dryers bought together with washing machines. Would you be interested in hearing about this?"

And just like that, Jordan had shown me in a very practical way how I could improve the metric I was to focus on: units per transaction. She moved me from buying a washing machine to considering a washer-dryer combination.

Best Buy sales associates all over Denver were receiving this tailored coaching weekly, with daily check-ins to discuss how they were doing. My executive coach, Marshall Goldsmith, often told me that coaching is a contact sport: to work, it has to be as frequent as it is practical, and that was the kind of coaching happening in Denver.

Note that, in this approach, the manager becomes a highly skilled coach. Unleashing human magic requires managers to be more than just managers. To be good coaches, the managers in Denver had to master the sales craft themselves.

This reminds me of a joke about parrots. A woman walks into a bird store and sees a parrot. "How much is this parrot?" she asks. "A hundred dollars," says the store owner. "This parrot is special: it can speak over a hundred words, make coffee, and read the newspaper." The customer nods and sees another parrot, which sells for a thousand dollars. That parrot, explains the store owner, is even more special: it speaks five languages, makes a full breakfast, and delivers press briefings. There is a third parrot, however. When she asks how much that parrot costs, the customer is shocked to find out that it costs $10,000. What could this parrot possibly do to justify such a premium? "No one knows," the store owner replies. "But the other two call it 'boss.'"

Reassessing Performance Assessments and Development

When I joined EDS France in 1996, the majority of the staff was not receiving any formal regular feedback. Many of our team members had no opportunity to discuss how they might get better at what they did, let alone be coached. To put the People → Business → Finance philosophy into action, I decided that everyone would get an annual performance review and opted to assess managers partly on how well they themselves assessed their own team members.

Over the years, I have also learned that performance discussions are far more effective when leaders eschew the traditional top-down, grading approach.

First, having the subject do most of the work can be much more productive than having the manager do it. By the time I became CEO of Carlson in 2008, I had gone through my fair share of typical 360 reviews, ratings, and rankings and realized how pointless they were. Once a year, managers would sit with their direct reports, trying hard—and usually failing—to replay an entire year in their heads, telling them how well they did or did not do against a list of predefined criteria. Colleagues and reports would contribute their opinion. Salary increases would typically be tied to the outcome of these annual sit-downs, which poisoned the discussions by introducing financial consequences.

I still remember a protracted argument with one of my reports about his rating: he was convinced he deserved a five out of five, and I thought a three was more appropriate. We locked horns over that number, which in retrospect was ridiculous. Only 14 percent of employees feel that their performance reviews inspire them to improve, according to Gallup. In fact, traditional performance reviews are often so bad that in about a third of cases they make performance worse.[4] This is hardly the way to unleash human magic.

At Best Buy, I no longer personally rated and assessed my direct reports. Who is to say that you deserve a three or a five? Who says your supervisor can accurately evaluate and rate you? Instead, I encouraged people who reported directly to me to do self-assessments informed by feedback from their colleagues, to use that assessment to develop their own plans to grow, and then to share the whole thing with me. I have found that they were usually excellent at assessing their performance. I mainly ensured that we agreed on priorities and asked them how I could help them achieve their development goals. This is far more motivating than the traditional approach.

Second, performance management should be more about development than ranking. General Electric famously used to rank its employees annually and fired every year those deemed to be in the bottom 10 percent. Rankings, however, are often based on lofty criteria and subjective judgment, which is a problem. They also pit people against each other. And regardless of how good people might be at what they do, there is always a bottom 10 percent, which may lead to a loss of valuable talent.

Compare this to conductor Benjamin Zander's and therapist Rosamund Stone Zander's practice of "giving an 'A.'" While teaching at the New England Conservatory, Ben Zander watched how anxiety over grades stymied student after student. Afraid to fail, they were reluctant to take risks, which undermined the development of true mastery. Zander decided that each September, in the first class of a two-semester course on musical performance, he would announce upfront that all students would get an "A" for the course. There was one condition: within two weeks, each student had to write a letter dated the following May—the end of the course—explaining in detail what had happened during those months to justify that extraordinary grade. They had to project themselves in the future and look back at their accomplishment and learning, describing the person they had become. Freed from judgment, his students could imagine a world of possibility. The practice of giving an "A" upfront unleashed their energy and drive. They imagined themselves breaking through whatever it was that stood in their way—and did. Giving an "A" is not meant to ignore standards, competence, and accomplishment, but rather to align student and teacher—or manager and employee—in a common purpose: strive for mastery.[5]

"You can't manage people's behavior, and you can't manage their performance," says Kamy Scarlett, Best Buy's head of human resources. Instead, she argues, leaders support people's potential. In October 2019, Best Buy announced that it would replace annual top-down reviews and engagement surveys with quarterly conversations, led by employees, about their goals, progress, and development.

Third, performance development should be more about honing strengths than addressing problems. Managers conducting traditional performance reviews typically highlight three things going well and three development opportunities, based on a precooked list of attributes required for the job. Over time, I have embraced the idea that developing the individual means nurturing each person's unique talents so he or she can become even better—what authors Marcus Buckingham and Ashley Goodall call "spiky" people.[6] We do not need to be good at everything, which is not only unrealistic in real life, but also leads to dulling our areas of brilliance and inner drive. It is in coming together in all our diversity of talents and of what gives us the most joy that we create the best possible performance. Mastery does not come from working on your "weaknesses," but in relentlessly honing and leveraging your unique combination of strengths. It is, of course, a balancing act, but the focus on building strengths can lead to a more powerful outcome.

Treating Learning as a Lifelong Journey

As recounted earlier, I once looked askance at executive coaching. I believed training was for beginners, and coaching was remedial. At McKinsey, plenty of training was available at lower echelons, but no development was on offer for partners. Training for CEOs wasn't a thing either.

When the head of HR at Carlson first suggested I consider working with a coach, she explained that Marshall Goldsmith was helping successful CEOs become even better at what they did. Seen in that light, I was in. Who doesn't want to keep getting better at what they love doing? Psychologist and Stanford University professor Carol Dweck's "growth mindset" makes learning and improvement a lifelong pursuit.

I have learned to embrace mastery as lifelong growth. The best athletes in the world all work with coaches. Rafael Nadal and Roger Federer did not fire their coaches when they became tennis champions. Through coaching, I was able to become better at what I love doing. I have learned to appreciate and use feedback. I have learned to help people do their jobs rather than personally come up with the answers to solve problems. I have learned to become a leader who focused more on people than numbers. I have learned that my main job as CEO was to create and steer a purposeful human organization powered by human magic. I have learned that I will never stop learning and will keep striving to be better at what I do.

The road to mastery has no final destination: it is a never-ending journey.

Making Space for Failure

Management literature is replete with how important failure is. So, instead of just repeating the general idea, I want to add some personal color and specificity.

Best Buy's 2013 holiday season was a low point in our turnaround. We missed our targets, and stores' sales were lower than the previous year's. The stock price, which had almost quadrupled over the previous year, from $11 to $42, immediately sank 30 percent.

We had a choice: we could either look for excuses and culprits, or we could learn and move forward. How did we want to react?

Before making any public announcement to the market, I gathered Best Buy's 100 most senior leaders. I borrowed from some of my favorite movies to make my point. "Why do we fall, Bruce?" asks the father of the boy who would later become Batman in the 2005 movie *Batman Begins*. "So that we can learn to pick ourselves up." During the meeting, I also showed a scene from *Any Given Sunday*, during which Al Pacino gives a classic inspirational speech to his football team at halftime, after a crushing first half. "We're in hell right now," he tells the players, "and we can stay here, get the shit kicked out of us, or we can fight our way back into the light. We can climb out of hell. One inch at a time."

Then I asked everyone to write a memo detailing what each one of us, myself included, could have done differently. We shared what we wrote with one another, but not as a witch hunt. Instead, we tried to understand what had gone wrong and how we could improve. We discovered, for example, that when it had become clear that the season wasn't going well, our changing stores opening hours and introducing last-minute promotions just before Christmas only created confusion.

Jeff Bezos distinguishes between two types of failure. The first is failing to execute in areas of well-established expertise. For Amazon, that might be opening a new warehouse. There should be little tolerance for failures that relate to the core business. The second, on the other hand, happens when exploring new ideas and new ways of doing things, which is essential to innovation. Failure there is to be expected and embraced.

Leadership can encourage the second type of failure by explicitly stating that it's safe. This is what the "get-out-of-jail-free" cards I distributed to Best Buy's senior leaders were about: encouraging experimentation. The key is to protect the downside and to take calculated, reversible gambles. This was the approach our strategic growth office adopted with initiatives like the in-house advisors: come up with new ideas, design pilots, test them, then either shelve them or roll them out more widely. In fact, the first pilot for in-home advisors failed, and we had to go back to the drawing board and try again. Likewise, when we decided to match online prices early in our turnaround, it was initially an experiment we could have reversed had it not paid off. Many pilots did not succeed, and we ended up shelving ideas like providing broadband access to apartment buildings or offering assortments tailored for specific rooms in the house. Without these failed experiments, we would not have developed the successful ones.

. . .

Connecting individual purposes with the company's, nurturing authentic human connections, encouraging autonomy, fostering mastery—they all contribute to creating an environment in which every individual wants to give the best of him- or herself, which, in the context of an appropriate strategy, unleashes extraordinary results.

There is one more thing, though. Think of contraction or stagnation. Do you feel inspired? Neither do I. Few people, if anyone, ever do. Which leads us to the fifth ingredient of human magic: growth.

Questions to Reflect On

- Think of something you love doing. What do you tend to focus on more: effort or result?

- Do you feel that your own professional development fits your situation? And how individualized is your direct reports' development?

- How prevalent is coaching in your company?

- How do you assess the performance of your direct reports?

- How is your own performance evaluated? By whom? Do you find it motivating?

- What do you feel you are doing well? And what would you like to become better at professionally? What is your plan to improve?

- What is your most spectacular failure? Was it related to a core activity or an innovative experiment? What have you learned from it?

13

Fifth Ingredient: Putting the Wind at Your Back

Growth is the only evidence of life.

—Cardinal John Henry Newman

When considering Jim Citrin's not-so-crazy idea to become the CEO of Best Buy, I listened to half a dozen of the company's past earnings calls and meetings with investors. They all shared one recurring theme: Best Buy's problems were due to "headwinds." Best Buy, the story went, was gaining shares in key categories. But alas! The market environment for consumer electronics was a problem. So was the shift to online shopping and the fact that Amazon was not collecting sales tax. Apple Stores added to the headwinds. Prices on key products were deflating; the iPhone was making cameras, voice recorders, and music players redundant.

Best Buy appeared to be the victim of a perfect storm of circumstances—even the best sailors cannot overcome such headwinds. But how could that be? All my previous jobs had been in industries where IT and electronics played a positive role. The likes of Amazon, Apple, and Samsung were doing very well.

In one of my first addresses at Best Buy, I asked the company's top leaders to imagine how the conversation would go if I were to call Apple's CEO Tim Cook and Amazon's Jeff Bezos.

"How is the wind where you are sailing?" I would ask.

"The wind is great! Great sailing. We're having the time of our life," they both would answer. So if they found the wind at their backs, I concluded, then the problem was not the wind. And if wind was not the problem, then *we* probably were. We could keep coming up with the best possible excuses and wait for the unlikely day when prizes would be handed out in that category. Or we could change tack.

First, we had to regroup, which required some pruning. There are times when shrinking is necessary—very much like Michelangelo chipping away at his block of marble to remove all that was not his statue. During Best Buy's turnaround, we decided to exit the Chinese and European markets. We consolidated two brands in Canada under the Best Buy banner.

Once the turnaround was over, we faced a choice: Should Best Buy embrace the pruning and focus on becoming a smaller, more profitable company? Or had the pruning been a tactical move so we could step toward new strategic horizons to unleash new growth?

For me then—and now—growth is an imperative. It creates space for promotion opportunities, productivity improvement without job loss, taking risks, and investing. Business growth fosters individual growth and drive, which in turn feeds back into innovation and further business expansion.

As such, growth is the fifth and final essential ingredient of unleashing human magic. It is hard to feel energized, creative, and ready to take risks in a context of stagnation, contraction, fear, uncertainty, or doubt. A sense of endless possibilities—both for oneself and for the business in pursuit of a noble purpose—fuels inner drive, positive energy, and the desire to bring one's best self to the table.

If you are supposedly facing "headwinds" and oppression in your current market, you tack to put the wind at your back by:

- Thinking in terms of possibilities

- Turning challenges to your advantage

- Keeping purpose front and center

Thinking Possibilities

In 2017, we were elaborating our strategy and preparing our upcoming presentation to investors when Asheesh Saksena, who had taken over the strategic growth unit from Corie Barry after she became CFO, proposed that we redefine what we considered our market. Best Buy had until then narrowly defined it as the retail sale of the physical hardware offered in our stores. So, the sale of DVDs, for example, was part of that market. But video streaming was not. In his presentation to the executive team, Asheesh had broadened the boundaries by including the total spend on consumer technology, including services and subscriptions, for each of the human needs we had decided Best Buy would address.

Seen in this light, our market was no longer defined as what Best Buy was already doing, but rather as what it could potentially do. From a universe worth some $250 billion, we were now looking at a market worth over $1 trillion. His vision opened a world of possibilities.

But when he first showed it, the gasps in the room were nearly audible. It made the team nervous. They worried that until we knew for sure we could deliver in these new areas and capture a portion of any of these new-to-us markets, we risked losing credibility.

Asheesh's thinking was shocking to many because he wasn't bound by market share, the metric most often used to define business strategy and success. Yet, just as it is with a pie, focusing on getting a bigger slice of an existing market is a narrow and ultimately self-defeating approach to business. Your piece only grows when another's shrinks. Companies seeking to be "the best" or "number one" play a constricted zero-sum game—and are likely one day to find themselves on the losing side.

For Asheesh, the headwinds related to hardware being sold in stores were hardly out of our control. Why not just expand our field of vision to redefine our market and unlock latent demand to grow— what authors Chan Kim and Renée Mauborgne call the Blue Ocean strategy?[1] Once we adopt this expansive view of markets and industries, everybody can grow. This is a much more positive perspective. Instead of obsessing about crushing the competition, companies focus on striving to be the best versions of themselves, guided by their own unique purpose and their own unique assets.

Microsoft CEO Satya Nadella embodies this mindset. Every year, Microsoft organizes a summit of some 200 CEOs of the largest US companies, from JP Morgan to Berkshire Hathaway. When I attended this conference before Satya became CEO, the only technology in sight at that summit was Microsoft's own. The demos of the company's software would always be on its own hardware, even smartphones— not an area where the Microsoft star shone the brightest. Systematically focusing on how well the suite of Microsoft products worked together, which suggested that they should only operate together, narrowed the company's perspective.

When I again attended the summit in 2014, Satya, who had become CEO a few months earlier, demonstrated Microsoft's new software on Apple's iPhones. Suddenly, the company's horizons had opened up to the universe of iOS and Android, far broader than the market share of Microsoft's own phones. That kind of spirit has the power to transform people, and therefore companies. Not surprisingly, Microsoft's culture opened up, speed of execution vastly increased, and its share price skyrocketed under Satya's leadership.

Asheesh Saksena was right to suggest that we stretch Best Buy's market definition to focus on what was possible, but adopting that mindset is not easy. Pushback was swift from people who had just been through a turnaround, during which there had been no room for error and little appetite for risk. Redefining our market carried risks of overpromising and failing. Yet we had to take risks to pivot from survival to growth. When we presented to our investors that year, we adopted Asheesh's new market vision. We had to change how we set our objectives and how we planned.

In a turnaround, you draw a plan that you are almost certain to fulfill. Sharon McCollam, who was Best Buy's CFO during our turn-around years, was a master at this approach. She ensured that we would not miss financial targets, which earned her immense respect and credibility from the market watchers monitoring our every move.

For growth, another kind of planning is in order. It's exemplified by Kurt Ritter, who led the Rezidor Hotel Group when I was Carlson's CEO. Kurt mobilized his team around BHAGs—big hairy audacious goals—that capture the imagination even though no one quite knows how to get there.[2] Kurt's BHAG was to add a breathtaking number of hotel rooms to the company's portfolio, and Rezidor was in fact one of the fastest-growing hotel companies in the world.

Fostering an expansive mindset and a sense of possibility year after year requires striking the right balance between both these ap-proaches. To inspire drive and motivation, goals should be ambitious. Unrealistic overstretches, on the other hand, can demoralize and breed skepticism. Systematically missing targets hurts the manage-ment team's credibility with investors and with employees, who grow tired of not achieving what they set out to and, more prosaically, of missing out on bonuses.

The rollout of Best Buy's in-home advisor program struck that balance. It was an audacious leap into services, but how big a leap should it be? We could either adopt a narrow approach, starting from the number of stores we had, making assumptions on how many advisors we should have per store, and extrapolating from there. In this scenario, we would plan for a few hundred advisors.

Alternatively, we could forget how many stores we had, and instead start with the number of households in the market; estimate what proportion could use some technology and a Best Buy advisor; and figure out how many households a single advisor could serve. When taking that perspective, the number of in-home advisors could easily reach 5,000 to 10,000. The number itself, though, is less important than the perspective it represents. I did not suggest that we should immediately start recruiting, training, and deploying thousands of advisors. It would take time to successfully roll out our new program. It is a balancing act. To embark on this journey, the key is to dream big and start small.

Over time, we became better at discerning and unlocking new possibilities. Assembling an executive team who embraced that perspective and vision, combined with setting up operational bolsters such as the strategic growth office to realize that vision, made that shift possible. By 2019, Best Buy's new CEO, Corie Barry, laid out the company's growth strategy with stretch targets for people, business, and finance, to be met by 2025. The turnaround mindset had given way to an expansive sense of possibility and growth.

Turning Challenges to Your Advantage

In 1805, Napoleon and his formidable troops were camped at Boulogne in Northern France, ready to attack England. On October 21, however, the British navy delivered a crushing defeat on the combined

French and Spanish naval force at Trafalgar. The debacle was a significant setback for Napoleon: without control of the English Channel, his planned invasion of England was no longer possible.

Napoleon turned challenge into opportunity. He redirected his Boulogne troops eastward, covering some 1,300 kilometers in less than six weeks. He then crushed the Austrian and Russian imperial forces in Austerlitz in what is still considered one of the greatest military actions of all time. Prussian general and military strategist Carl von Clausewitz ascribed Napoleon's military success, on top of his speed of action, to his *coup d'oeil*, or glance—the ability to see the big picture in simple and clear terms, and by doing so, to detect opportunities beyond apparent limitations or challenges.

The ability to see what's possible in simple terms and to rally people around it is particularly essential when facing immediate challenges. What stops most of us from being able to do this are those gale-force headwinds, which can be so disheartening, daunting, and paralyzing. Yet it is in these situations that leaders have to mobilize and energize teams by carving pathways around these obstacles, and embrace the opportunity to overcome adversity.

When I became CEO of Best Buy, I was often asked why on earth I had taken on a job that many saw as a lost cause. The truth is I love challenges; they give me energy. Part of it is the satisfaction and adrenaline that comes from building and mobilizing a team around a common goal and solving a puzzle. It is a chance for me to fulfill my purpose, which is to make a positive difference on people around me and use the platform I have to make a positive difference in the world.

This is the kind of energy I experienced at EDS France, Vivendi Games, Carlson Wagonlit Travel, and Carlson. When I started at EDS, the company, whose business in the United States was built on securing long-term outsourcing megadeals, was struggling in France, where such megadeals were not in favor, and losing revenues fast. Working with our team to find a way to succeed in the French market and mobilizing everyone at the company around this was immensely energizing. Helping Vivendi Games solve its challenges—and its key division Blizzard Entertainment to succeed internationally—was exciting too. So was revitalizing Carlson Wagonlit Travel at a time when internet travel booking was supposed to kill the business.

The Covid-19 pandemic that swept across the world in 2020 created significant challenges, threatening the survival of many companies. Yet the severe constraints around health and safety also offered new possibilities. Being forced to rethink process, products, and services brought about new ways to tap into unexplored demand and unleash new growth.

Before the Covid-19 crisis, for example, Adobe, the digital creativity company, would hold an annual conference in Las Vegas for 15,000 attendees. In 2020, they could not physically gather because of social distancing and safety concerns. They held their conference digitally and got *80,000* people to attend, as travel and finding a facility that could hold such a large group were no longer constraints.

Or think about Ralph Lauren. At the corner of Madison Avenue and 72nd Street in Manhattan is "the Mansion," Ralph Lauren's flagship store in New York City. New Yorkers and tourists alike love to browse within the wood-paneled temple to the founder's vision of timeless style. During the Covid-19 epidemic, the company promptly closed all its stores to protect staff and customers. Yet as the Mansion's physical doors closed, virtual ones opened. Customers were still able to experience the store via online video chats with salespeople. In fact, this expanded the store's customer base beyond those who were proximate to a retail outlet. In a different space, think how remote learning can allow an education institution to reach a much larger population, or how much easier it becomes to have extraordinary guest speakers in what has become a virtual classroom.

Besides expanding reach, the Covid-19 crisis has also created opportunities to transform customer experience. In April 2020, Best Buy decided to reopen some of its stores, which the company had closed in March, for one-on-one consultations by appointment. This took care of safety concerns related to excessive crowds in a store and provided a high-touch experience to customers. It also led to a higher sales close rate, as the shoppers who made an appointment were those actively looking for solutions and keen to pay for them, rather than browsers.

In the same vein, the Covid-19 crisis and the associated safety concerns gave telemedicine a long-awaited boost, which technological progress has facilitated. Telemedicine allows medical practitioners, for certain conditions, to see patients from the comfort of their home. This frees patients from having to travel to a hospital or their MD's office at a time when they least want to move.

Keeping Purpose Front and Center

As discussed in chapter 5, articulating your company's noble purpose is a strategic imperative. But just as importantly, purpose also helps create an expansive mindset and a sense of possibility, particularly in tough times. When Best Buy thought of itself as a chain of stores selling consumer electronics, the world was full of headwinds. When it defined its purpose as enriching the lives of customers through technology, however, it inspired the company's people to see new markets that could make a meaningful and enduring difference in people's lives. This is what I meant when I told investors in 2017 that Best Buy is not in the commodities business, but in the happiness business. The formulation of the company's purpose has opened up the opportunity to stand the test of time and weather business, market, and technological changes. The purpose is a horizon line you never reach. Twenty or 30 years from now, technology will still offer opportunities to enrich people's lives, regardless of whether there are holographic stores or drones delivering products.

Crises such as the Covid-19 pandemic force us to focus on purpose to expand our perspective. The Minneapolis Institute of Art closed its doors during the worst of the crisis. But fulfilling its mission to "inspire wonder through the power of art" was not confined to the museum's four walls. Driven by the museum's purpose, its staff launched a flurry of activities that allowed anyone with an internet connection to explore the museum's collection from home, listen to podcasts, and attend virtual events. The museum has therefore been able to inspire wonder in new ways and within a much wider audience, freed from constraints of proximity and physical access.

Restaurants that have developed a pickup or delivery service, or even a new business around delivering the food ingredients that allow customers to re-create their most beloved recipes at home, illustrate the same idea. Focusing on a broader purpose allows them to reach a population in excess of their seating capacity.

·   ·   ·

In a popular French comic book centered on two characters named Asterix and Obelix, a small village in Brittany accomplishes the seemingly impossible in 50 B.C.: it stands against the mighty Roman empire, which, having subjugated the rest of Gaul, fails time and time again to invade the village. The village's weapon is its druid's secret potion, which gives whoever drinks it superhuman strength.

Performance defying all expectations is not confined to comic books. It can happen in business as well. But as with Asterix, it requires human magic. Unlike with Asterix, however, the potion that produces these results is not secret. It takes five ingredients, all of which were presented here in part three.

A new perspective on work discussed in part one; the architecture of a purposeful human organization presented in part two; and part three's human magic ingredients, though, do not quite add up to the refoundation of business. It takes one more thing: a new kind of leader.

Questions to Reflect On

- Are you operating in a world of possibilities or constraints?

- How have you defined your and your organization's goal? Is your goal to be number one or to be the best you can be?

- Are you able to redefine the possibilities for yourself and your organization?

- How do challenges tend to affect you? Do they drain you? Energize you?

- How do you connect your growth strategy with your purpose?

Part Four

THE CASE FOR PURPOSEFUL LEADERSHIP

The view of business presented in this book is based on a different approach to work (part one), an alternative view of the role and nature of companies (part two), and a perspective on the environment necessary to unleash irrational performance (part three). To bring all these elements together, we must shift traditional views of leadership. This is what part four is about. The model of the leader as a smart, powerful, superhero is outdated. Today's leaders have to be purposeful, be clear about whom they serve, be conscious of what their true role is, be driven by values, and be authentic—the five "Be's" of the purposeful leader.

14

How We Lead Matters

You have chosen wisely.

—Grail Knight, in *Indiana Jones and the Last Crusade*

In 2000, when I led Vivendi's video games division, parent company Vivendi acquired media giant Universal. I e-mailed my boss arguing why I should be part of the team that would lead the integration of the two companies. I had worked on managing post-merger situations at McKinsey, I wrote; I had the right skills. It worked. I was selected to lead the effort that would "extract synergies" from the merger in the United States. I was to report directly to Vivendi's chief operating officer in Paris. My appointment was announced in a press release following a board meeting. I was very excited.

Did I feel that my new job was fulfilling a noble purpose or that I would be making a positive difference in the world? Honestly, these questions were not on my mind. I must confess I put myself forward out of personal ambition. I was happy because I felt my new job took me one step closer to the top.

My excitement was short-lived, though. There were not many syner-gies to extract. Universal's mostly US-based business, which included music, a movie studio, and theme parks, did not overlap much with Vi-vendi's largest businesses—mobile phone and pay TV services, based mainly in France. Letting my ego drive my decisions, I landed a job that was at once prestigious and largely pointless. Ultimately, the job brought me little joy, as I dragged myself from meeting to meeting, encouraging and monitoring largely meaningless activities. Fortunately, it ended within 18 months. By 2002, Vivendi's acquisition spree had left the com-pany saddled with too much debt, plunging the company into crisis. I became part of the team that led the restructuring of the company.

Vying for the post-merger job at Vivendi taught me a valuable lesson: be aware—and beware—of what drives you. It forced me to ask myself what kind of leader I wanted to be. Ever since, I have tried to measure up future career choices with a different yardstick. Is it aligned with my purpose? Will I be able to make a significant positive contribution in this role? Will I enjoy it? In other words, is this oppor-tunity going to be meaningful, impactful, and joyful? These were the questions I asked myself when considering becoming CEO of Best Buy. People thought I was crazy, but to me the role met these three crucial criteria.

The choice of what kind of leader we want to be is one of the two most critical choices we get to make. The second is: Who else should we put in a position of leadership?

I grew up influenced by three ideas about leadership that have shaped how I initially thought about the answer to these questions and the business world more broadly:

- Leaders are some kind of superheroes.

- Leadership is an innate capability.

- People cannot change.

Time and experience have proven to me these are myths and that we get to choose the kind of leader we want to be. That choice matters immensely for the organizations and people we lead.

Debunking Three Myths about Leadership

Myth 1: Leaders are superheroes

Growing up, I thought successful leaders saved the day largely on their own, by figuring out the answers. Being smart—and making sure everyone else knew it—seemed to be the mark of the best leaders. The best schools were supposed to lead to the best jobs, which produced the best leaders. Power, fame, glory, and money were the measures of professional success. And truthfully, these considerations influenced some of my early career choices.

During my last year of business school, I was invited to the dean's office, where I was offered a job assisting the chairman and CEO of Sacilor, a large state-owned steel company. My predecessor in the job, who was by then ready to climb the next rung on the well-defined career ladder, had been, like me, class valedictorian. I accepted the job immediately, not out of a sense of purpose, but because the job was prestigious, and the connections it would bring would help my career. I was taking my first step toward the rarefied circle of France's business elite, made up of smart graduates from a handful of top schools who became those powerful hero-leaders, the smartest people in the room.

The idea of a brilliant hero-leader who single-handedly saves the day is deeply rooted, reaching back to ancient Greece and all its powerful demigods, with Hercules the most prominent one, and extending all the way forward to business today. Early in my career, prominent business leaders like GE's Jack Welch were revered for their intellect, strategic sense, and hard-charging style. They were considered infallible geniuses, inspiring a quasi-cult following.

Recently, though, the infallible leader prototype has lost much of its appeal. First, an increasing number of people now value authenticity and connection. Research by Paula Niedenthal, professor of psychology at the University of Wisconsin–Madison, points out that we are wired to detect inauthenticity.[1] And projecting infallibility, strength, and authority at all times—something that for decades has been expected of leaders—comes across as inauthentic and distant. Second, the hero-leader model fails to take into account the idea of purpose, which is central to business. Superheroes belong in movies, not in business.

Third, it is easy for successful hero-leaders to start believing in the myth that they are smarter than everyone else, untouchable, and ultimately indispensable. It is easy to be seduced by power, fame, glory, and money. It is easy to become disconnected from reality and from colleagues, surrounded by sycophants and yea-sayers. Matt Furman, in charge of Best Buy's communications, perfectly sums up that mindset: "Enough about me," he jokes. "Now let's talk about me!"

History is littered with celebrity CEOs once seen as business geniuses or superheroes, who have moved from the cover of magazines to prison cells, from Enron's Jeff Skilling and Nissan's Carlos Ghosn to Qwest's Joseph Nacchio and WorldCom's Bernie Ebbers.

The years I spent wrestling with feedback and letting personal ambition drive some earlier career decisions illustrate how I used to gravitate toward that mythical superhero CEO model. Once I realized this was not the kind of leader I wanted to be, I actively decided to protect myself against this trap. "Your mission is to make sure I am never on the cover of any magazine," I instructed the communications team when I became the CEO of Best Buy. I insisted on flying commercial for as long as I could. I set up guardrails to keep my feet on the ground. I wanted to make sure that my ego would not get the best of me.

"I am not the CEO of Best Buy," I said, shortly after I joined the company, in a column in the local Minneapolis newspaper. What I meant was that although I was honored to have the job, it did not define me. My goal from the very start was to be dispensable. This is why I decided to pass the baton of CEO to Corie Barry and her team in 2019. I felt I had accomplished what I had set out to do, and it was an easy decision. The company was doing well, powered by exceptional people and led by an extraordinary executive team. Hero-leaders believe in being out in front, highly visible. In the case of leadership transitions, I would say that a key to success is *not* being visible. Be available in the background, only if and when needed. After a year, the transition was complete, and I stepped down as executive chairman. Because I never defined myself as the CEO of Best Buy, it has been easy to move on.

Myth 2: People are born leaders

When Lloyd Blankfein was still CEO of investment bank Goldman Sachs, I heard a speech he once gave at the Minneapolis Club. Blankfein shared with us that, every day while shaving, he asked himself, "Is it today? Is it today that the world is going to realize that I am not competent for this job?" Here was one of the most successful bankers in the world, and he was doubting his own abilities. Most leaders I know—myself included—suffer from the same imposter syndrome.

That syndrome is born in part out of the misguided belief that leadership is an innate ability, emerging out of a level of intelligence, self-confidence, and charisma that you're born either with or without. If it were true, there would be just a few exceptional beings who could do the job, and the rest of us would be out of luck. Research suggests it's not true, though; so do the narratives of great leaders' lives. Iconic figures such as Winston Churchill hardly fit the mold of the flawless born leader, spawn fully formed and ready to inspire. Early in life, Churchill was a notoriously poor student and suffered from a speech impediment. Later on, he became one of the most prominent leaders of the twentieth century. Yes, *became*. I believe that most of the attributes often associated with "innate" leadership—from strategic thinking to eloquence—can be learned. As recounted in earlier chapters, coaching and role models have helped me become a better leader throughout my career.

Myth 3: You cannot change

During my time at Best Buy, one of our executives once told me she was convinced that people do not and cannot change. I vehemently disagreed because I am living proof that people change. The way I lead today is remarkably different from the way I led 30 years ago. I once believed that leadership was about a top-down, strategic planning approach driven by data and analytics; I now focus on purpose and human magic. I once strove to be the smartest person in the room and solve all problems; I now focus on creating an environment in which others can flourish and find solutions. And I used to believe that profit was the purpose of business; I now know that it is only an imperative and an outcome.

Becoming the Leader You Choose to Be

As I eventually concluded that leaders are neither born nor superhumans, I realized that I was free to decide what kind of leader I would be. My choice, obviously critical to me, would also influence how I interact with others and reverberate through organizations by way of the people I put in place to lead others.

There were so many models to choose from: bookshelves are full of leadership books advocating different approaches with different leadership labels.[2] Clayton Christensen gave this advice to graduating Harvard Business School students in 2010: "Think about the metric by which your life will be judged, and make a resolution to live every day so that in the end, your life will be judged a success."[3] This is a good framing to me. To make a choice about the kind of leader you want to be, think about three things: what drives you, the legacy you want to leave, and how to stay the course.

What drives you?

In the fall of 2018, I spent a Sunday afternoon in Midtown Manhattan attending one of designer Ayse Birsel's workshops—Design the Life You Love. Ayse encourages people to use principles of design to think about life choices. In one particularly profound exercise, she asked us to think about the people we admired. My list was a diverse group of individuals, from Gandhi to former Medtronic CEO Bill George. Ayse told us to write down the qualities that made us admire the people on our list. My list of attributes seemed to center on the will and ability to make a big difference in the world and an unwavering commitment to support and help others.

"This is what you want to be," Ayse then told us. It was up to us to embrace these qualities as our own and to act accordingly.

The timing of this exercise was perfect. I had started thinking about moving on from Best Buy. Although the purpose I had identified during the Loyola spiritual exercises all these years before remained the same, Ayse's workshop helped me further crystallize the qualities that were important to me and be bolder about taking them to what I would do next.

What legacy do you want to leave?

Second, it is worth investing time to reflect on that question and making sure that your decisions and how you spend your time, efforts, and energy reflect that choice. How do you get that kind of clarity?

Executive leadership coach and author Hortense le Gentil routinely asks her clients to write their obituary. This is a powerful way to focus their minds on what they want to accomplish and whether the choices they are making are aligned with that purpose. Similarly, during Harvard Business School's workshop for new CEOs, professor Michael Porter asks participants to write their retirement speech. How do they want to be remembered? What do they want their contribution to be? What kind of legacy do they want to leave?

Of course, when asked these questions, few executives ever highlight how much money they will have made, how many people they have fired, or how many times they have appeared on the cover of magazines.

How do you stay the course?

Christensen pointed out in his speech to MBA graduates that no successful executive sets out to go to jail. But high achievers have a propensity to unconsciously allocate their time and energy to what yields short-term tangible accomplishment and recognition rather than to what and who they would say matters the most.[4] Correcting for such propensities requires self-awareness and a daily routine to help you keep in touch with yourself. Marshall Goldsmith encourages his clients to write down a list of questions about behaviors reflecting important values and ask themselves *every day* whether they have done their best to act that way. Whatever form of introspection you choose, hit the "pause" button every day to make sure you stay in touch with your purpose and live by it. Besides self-awareness and firmly holding on to your principles, we can choose to rely on family, friends, colleagues, a coach, a mentor, or a good board of directors to act as guardrails that help us stay on course—or get back on track if we slip up.

. . .

I no longer believe that my role as a leader is to figure it all out.

Choosing why and how to exercise power, and whom to give it to, are the most crucial choices leaders have to make. The notion that companies are human organizations made of individuals working together in pursuit of a common purpose implies that we need to change what we expect of leaders, at all levels.

What is required now is a style of leadership that puts purpose and people first, what I call purposeful leadership.

Questions to Reflect On

- What kind of a leader do you think you are today?

- What has driven your career decisions so far?

- What kind of leader do you want to be?

- How do you want to be remembered?

15

The Purposeful Leader

We can do so much more. We can save this
world with the right leadership.

—Adrian Veidt, *Watchmen*, 2009

In January 2013, Shari Ballard, Best Buy's then-head of human resources and stores, encouraged me to articulate what I thought made
a great leader. If the most important decision CEOs make is to choose
whom they put in a position of leadership, she argued, we had to be
clear about the criteria we would rely on to make these decisions. Our
turnaround plan was just getting underway, however, and Best Buy
was still in critical condition. I felt we should focus on action rather
than words, so I declined to go through the exercise back then.

But Shari was right, of course. And a few years later, after we had
saved the company and embarked on a growth strategy, she urged me
again to share my leadership principles. The time felt right. I had further clarified all the thoughts that I had formed, not just at Best Buy
but over two decades leading companies, about what I consider purposeful leadership.

These thoughts have shone throughout this book. Distilled to their essence, I think of them as the five "Be's" of purposeful leadership.

1. Be clear about your purpose, the purpose of people around you, and how it connects with the purpose of the company

When recruiting leaders, I used to ask candidates about their experience and the skills they had developed over time, their career goals, and whether they would be a good fit for the organization. Standard criteria. These felt like the most important considerations.

Now, I remember Marilyn Carlson Nelson on that flight from Paris to Minneapolis, asking me about my soul, and I spend more time seeking to understand a candidate's dreams and purpose. "What gives you energy?" I ask. "What drives you?"

"My purpose," says Corie Barry, my successor as CEO at Best Buy, "is to leave something a little better than when I found it—and that's true in my community, in my family and at Best Buy." Corie is very clear about her own purpose in life and how it connects with Best Buy's mission to enrich lives through technology. Before becoming CEO, she was instrumental in shepherding the company into new directions such as health care, which were in line with her own as well as Best Buy's purpose.

Now listed among the most powerful women by Fortune magazine and one of the youngest Fortune 500 CEOs, her purpose has not changed. She stays connected to it by asking herself, as she drives home from work every day, how things at Best Buy were a little better that day because she was there.

Now that I have stepped down as chairman and CEO of Best Buy, the question of purpose—not only one's own, but just as importantly, understanding what drives other people—is often part of the discussions I have with leaders that I coach. Recently, a successful CEO needed help with members of his team. He felt they were siloed, working primarily to advance their own functional area rather than the organization as a whole. Together, we realized that, although he was clear on his own purpose and his organization's, he didn't know much about what drove the people around him. Without that knowledge, it would be hard for him to help them connect their own purposes with the organization's, and provide a common, overarching pull for all team members.

During the Covid-19 pandemic, many of the business leaders I spoke with saw the crisis as a key moment for them to be clear about their purpose and connect it to their company's. The opportunity was there to help others and lead with humanity. They understood, to put it in Churchillian terms, that this could be and should be their "finest hour," and they wanted to rise to the occasion. They knew that their performance would be judged by how their company and its leadership were fulfilling a higher purpose and looking after its multiple stakeholders, not by the company's share price or whether it was hitting its earnings-per-share guidance.

2. Be clear about your role as a leader

In 2014, two weeks before Black Friday—one of the busiest days of the year for any retailer—law enforcement authorities contacted Best Buy to tell us we might have suffered a data breach. This was potentially catastrophic, and I was deeply concerned. We were still in the turnaround, and a data breach could torpedo the entire holiday season and the Renew Blue campaign. Early the next morning, I gathered our crisis management team, including representatives from IT and operations, legal, communications, finance, and more, in a small windowless conference room. We sat around a long table. The mood was somber. What should I do? Vent anger and frustration? Should I dive into problem solving?

I pushed all these thoughts aside and reminded myself to be a thermostat, rather than a thermometer, and set the temperature, in this case to upbeat and positive.

"No one would wish this two weeks before Black Friday," I said, "but this is an incredible leadership moment, and we get to decide how we live it. It gives us an opportunity to make a big difference and be the best version of ourselves—starting with myself. You are all incredibly qualified and talented, and I look forward to working with each one of you so we can create the best possible outcome. Now let's get on with it."

We had previously rehearsed what we would do if such a breach ever occurred, so we felt prepared. Luckily, the FBI's call turned out to be a false alarm; there was no data breach. But it was a good reminder that my role as a leader was to create energy and momentum—especially when circumstances are dire. It was to help others see possibilities and potential. Creating energy, inspiration, and hope: I would have dismissed this idea 30 years ago, but it is essential to the role of purposeful leader. Put another way, supposedly by John Quincy Adams: "If your actions inspire others to dream more, learn more, do more and become more, you are a leader."

You cannot choose circumstances, but you can control your mindset. Your mindset determines whether you generate hope, inspiration, and energy around you—or bring everyone down. So, choose well. I was reminded of this every morning when I worked at Carlson. A statue of Curt Carlson, the company founder, stood in the lobby of the company's headquarters, engraved with the words *Illegitimi non carborundum*—mock Latin best translated as "Don't let the bastards grind you down."

3. Be clear about whom you serve

"If you believe you're serving yourself, your boss, or me as the CEO of the company, it's okay—it's your choice," I once said to the officers of

Best Buy. "But then you should not work here. You should be promoted to customer." I meant that there was no room at Best Buy for people whose main purpose was to advance their career. One smart executive, who was recruited on the basis of his expertise and experience, ended up leaving Best Buy in large part because his personal ambition drove him. That he was primarily serving himself put him at odds with his colleagues.

Some leaders think that having sharp elbows and listening to their ego will serve their career. But is this the kind of person you want to be? Is this a choice you have to make? The best leaders do not climb to the top, says my friend Jim Citrin, who leads Spencer Stuart's CEO practice: they are carried to the top. And serving others is how it happens.

As a leader, you must serve the people on the front lines, driving the business. You serve your colleagues. You serve your board of directors. You serve the people around you, first by understanding what they need to give their best, so you can do your best to support them.

Executive coach Marshall Goldsmith once told me to see everyone as a customer. The way you treat the airline employee or the waiter in a restaurant, for example, will greatly influence the service you receive. This is a lesson that a top executive in one of the companies where I used to work learned the hard way. He was once stuck in an airport after his flight had been canceled. While standing in line at the service desk, waiting to get rerouted, he lost his patience and marched to the front of the queue. "Do you know who I am?" he hissed to the person behind the desk.

"Ladies and gentlemen, I need your help," said the airline employee, addressing travelers in the queue. "We have a case of forgotten identity. This man here does not know who he is!"

It takes vigilance and a healthy dose of self-awareness to avoid sliding into the trap set by power, fame, glory, and money. Stumbling into ego or ambition and trying to leverage your position like the executive at the airport happens to the best of us. This is a trap I fell into when, motivated by my own ego and ambition, I vied for a prestigious but largely meaningless job, as recounted in chapter 14. Before speaking or acting, be clear about your motivation and whom you are trying to serve.

4. Be driven by values

When I worked for McKinsey, I sought some leadership advice from one of my partners, Russ Fradin, who later became the lead independent director of the Best Buy board. "Tell the truth and do what's right," he said.

For the most part, we all agree on what is right: honesty, respect, responsibility, fairness, and compassion. On paper, every company has great values. But values are no good if they remain on paper. Being driven by values is doing right, not just knowing or saying what is right. A leader's role is to live by these values, explicitly promote them, and make sure they are part of the fabric of the business. Johnson & Johnson, for example, is famous for its Credo, first written in 1943 by the company founder's son. The company's decision in 1982 to immediately recall 31 million bottles of Tylenol, one of its bestselling products, after someone died from ingesting a tablet contaminated with cyanide, illustrates how the company leaders live by its Credo. Even today, the company regularly asks employees to rate how the company is living up to the Credo, and several rounds of Credo Challenges have nurtured open discussions around these values, questioned their relevance, and reinterpreted how they define the company in the present.

Similarly, both at Carlson and Best Buy, I established values days, during which every employee at the company would spend time discussing the company's values with their peers, debating how well we were living these values and what we could do to live them more fully.

Knowing and doing what is right is not always simple, of course. But Harvard Professor Clayton Christensen points out that it is easier to stick to your principles 100 percent of the time than it is to stick to them 98 percent of the time: the marginal cost of doing something that goes against your values "just this once" might appear temptingly low, but it may ultimately land you in jail, as the waters get muddier and muddier once the first exception gets made.[1] So, if you refuse to give in to the "just this once" and remember to tell the truth and do what's right, choices become easier.

Holding on to values is particularly critical during crises, when stress and pressure push against our sense of what's right. Harry Kraemer—the former chairman and CEO of health-care company Baxter International, professor of leadership at Kellogg, and an executive partner with the private equity firm Madison Dearborn—has voiced what many leaders felt during the Covid-19 crisis. "You're feeling worry, fear, anxiety, pressure, and stress. And these feelings completely overwhelm you. And as a result of basically becoming overwhelmed, you almost become incapacitated."

In his view, one of the main principles or mantras that leaders need to embrace to navigate crises is to believe that they are going to do the right thing, and do the best they can do. Kraemer acknowledges that doing the right thing is much more difficult than it sounds. But you don't have to figure it out on your own if you surround yourself with people you trust and whose values align with yours and the organization's. You will determine the right thing together and then act on it the best you can.[2]

I am proud of how values guided Best Buy's leadership during the Covid-19 crisis. In most states, Best Buy was deemed to provide an essential service—helping people working and learning from home to have the right equipment and support—which justified keeping stores open. Demand soared, but it had to be balanced with a more basic and fundamental priority: the safety and security of employees and customers. When employees worried about their safety and customers became understandably nervous, Corie and her team closed stores without hesitation. Within days, Best Buy pivoted its operating model to contactless curbside pickup. There was no way of knowing how closing down stores would impact the bottom line, but that didn't matter: what mattered was doing the right thing first.

Being driven by values also means knowing when to leave when you are not aligned with your environment—be it your colleagues, your boss, your board, or your company's values and purpose. Have the wisdom to know the difference between what you can and cannot change, the saying goes. I left EDS France largely because the new CEO's views on profit and people clashed with mine.

5. Be authentic

On June 11, 2020, I stepped down from my role as executive chairman of Best Buy. In many ways, it felt like a bigger step than passing the CEO baton the year before. Although I would keep cheering, admiring, and supporting Best Buy and its people, I no longer had any formal role at the company. After eight wonderful years, I emptied my office. Because the country was in the midst of the Covid-19 pandemic, I had to say goodbye electronically. "I love you!" was the title of the e-mail I sent to our senior leaders and our board members, with whom I had worked so closely. Above all, I wanted to express how I felt. And in the words of English writer A. A. Milne, I felt lucky to have something that made saying goodbye so hard. I shared similar emotions in a farewell video to all Best Buy employees. "Au revoir, my friends," I concluded. "I am keeping you in my heart."

Laying bare my heart and my soul in this way would have been unthinkable a few years ago. I have been told that the longest journey you'll ever take is the 18 inches between your head and your heart. It is a long and arduous journey indeed. Like many leaders of my generation, I long believed that emotions were not meant to be shared in a business context. I had a lot to unlearn, and it took me a lifetime to embrace the fifth, and for me by far the hardest, "Be": Be yourself, your true self, your whole self, the best version of yourself. Be vulnerable. Be authentic. This is something the new generation of leaders seems to grasp more intuitively and naturally.

We have all heard about the notion of work-life balance. Balancing family, friends, leisure, and work is an important consideration, but the wording suggests that life is outside of work, and work is something different than life, not our *real life*.

That notion evaporated during the Covid-19 pandemic, when so many people worked from home. We really brought our whole selves to work, including children, dogs, and cats. Our humanity was never more apparent. This is not always comfortable or easy. But we all had to see each other and show ourselves in a new light, in all our humanity.

Our employees are expecting us to be human, and they expect us to grasp who they are and to make them feel respected, heard, understood, and included. This means that we have to open up and make ourselves vulnerable, including by acknowledging what we do not know.

Brené Brown points out that vulnerability is at the heart of social connection. Social connection, in turn, is at the heart of business.

And it starts with each of us.

Questions to Reflect On

- Have you decided what kind of leader you want to be?

- How would you describe your purpose?

- What are you doing to create an environment in which others can thrive and flourish?

- Whom are you serving?

- What values define you?

- Are you doing your best to be authentic, approachable, and vulnerable?

CONCLUSION

A Call for Action

Dear Reader,

Where do we go from here?

What can each of us do to put purpose and people at the heart of business?

What can each of us do to truly unleash human magic and produce improbable results?

What can each of us do to amplify the movement toward the necessary refoundation of business and capitalism around the principles of purposeful and human leadership presented in this book?

These are important and urgent tasks. We need to act for the benefit of all stakeholders, for all the human beings who are citizens of this planet.

So, what will it take?

The good news is that the notions of purpose and stakeholder capitalism have been making strides within business circles in the United States and around the world. In my assessment, most leaders believe in this approach, at least at a high level. But I know from personal experience that there is a gap between understanding and doing. In my view, much remains to be done to turn thoughts and words into reality.

The refoundation I am calling for requires every one of us and each stakeholder group to change.

I like to say that the way you change behaviors is by changing behavior. So let's end this book by thinking about what we can do.

All of us have a role to play.

For Leaders

There is a story I love about a man who wanted to change the world. He first moved to Calcutta to help the poorest of the poor. But he was not happy. So he thought maybe he should move to New York and help the poor there. But still he was not happy. "Maybe I should take care of my family and help my wife and children the best I can," he thought. Yet he was not much happier. After a long period of reflection, he concluded that he should perhaps work on himself. So, he changed himself, and this is how he ended up changing the world.

To advance toward becoming the purposeful leader described in chapter 15, all of us must start with ourselves. To articulate and remain connected with what drives us requires introspection and reflection. We cannot be authentic and truly connect with others without deeply connecting with ourselves.[1] And to help people around us succeed and become the best version of themselves, we have to strive to be the best version of ourselves as well, day after day.

So, start with yourself.

Be the leader you are meant to be.

Be the change you want to see.

For Companies

Any farmer will tell you that seeds planted in poor soil do not grow. You first have to ensure that the soil is good.

The same holds true for companies. The first step for companies on their journey to pursue a noble purpose is not always to define the company's purpose. It may be more appropriate to first focus on creating a fertile environment, making sure that people feel that they exist, that they are seen, that they belong, that they matter. Only then can a noble purpose take root and flourish.

When the time is right, invest time to cocreate with your team a noble purpose at the intersection of (1) what the world needs; (2) the company's capabilities; (3) what drives people at the company, what they are passionate about, what they aspire to; and (4) how to make money.

Work with your team to translate the company's noble purpose into concrete strategic initiatives that can move the company forward meaningfully. Do that work before embarking on a communication mission. As marketing guru Ron Tite says, "Think. Do. Say." And when the time is right to communicate, articulate the noble purpose in words that are practical and straightforward enough for all employees at the company to understand what it concretely means for them and how they can write themselves into the story.

To be successful, the adoption of a new noble purpose will likely require a significant transformation of the company. It will likely require changing the way work gets done. This is not just about strategy but about changing the human side of the organization. It is about creating an environment where everyone can blossom and where human magic can be unleashed.

For Industry, Sector, and Community Leaders

Your impact extends beyond the four walls of your company. You are part of an ecosystem that includes your sector and your local community. Identify the systemic changes you can influence—for example, racial inequality, environmental issues—and tackle them with your peers. This is part of your job. Collective action, through industry initiatives, new norms, and improved standards, accelerates necessary change by leveling the competitive field.

For Boards of Directors

Ask yourself to what degree you approach your responsibilities in a way that aligns with these principles. To what extent

- does the way the company selects, evaluates, compensates, develops, and promotes leaders reflect principles of purposeful and human leadership?

- is the company's strategy anchored into a noble purpose in relation to all of its stakeholders in a meaningful fashion?

- does the way the company sets goals and manages performance reflect these principles?

- does the board help shape the culture of the company? Does it hold management accountable for creating an environment where everyone feels they belong and that represents the diversity of the company's customers and local community?

- do the company's policies, risk management and compliance programs align with the company's purpose and principles of purposeful, human leadership?

For Investors, Analysts, Regulators, and Rating Agencies

Ask yourself what else you can do to better align evaluation and investment decisions with principles of purposeful and human leadership.

Work has been done toward the development of new standards, norms, and tools that help evaluate how well a company is looking after *all* its stakeholders. The World Economic Forum and the Sustainability Accounting Standards Board, for example, have been advancing initiatives to incorporate sustainability measures into corporate performance assessment.

Further work is needed, however. For example, proxy advisory firms still focus exclusively on shareholder return when evaluating executive compensation. Accounting standards still do not incorporate externalities in evaluating economic performance.

For Business Education Institutions

A number of great institutions have begun to incorporate purpose and human dimensions into the education of tomorrow's leaders. They know that the best leaders are not going to be those who can best spell out the four Ps of marketing or calculate the net present value of an investment.

More needs to be done: How can we better help business students progress in their journey to become better, more purposeful, more aligned, more human leaders, and not superheroes? How can we teach students to anchor strategy into a noble purpose, to create environments in which others can be effective and inspired, and to tackle their responsibilities vis-à-vis all stakeholders?

. . .

Dear reader, it is up to each of us to carry this movement forward.

Now that I have left Best Buy and started a new chapter in my life, I am keen to add my voice and my energy to this cause. This is what has led me to write this book. This is why I decided three years ago to endow a chair on purposeful leadership at my alma mater in France, HEC Paris, and to collaborate with the faculty to advance the cause there. This is also why I have joined the faculty at Harvard Business School, where I am excited to support great colleagues to help educate the next generation of leaders. With my wife, executive leadership coach extraordinaire and acclaimed author Hortense le Gentil, I am also eager to support other leaders who are seeking to become the best version of themselves, lead from a place of purpose and humanity, and make a positive difference in the world.

How do you want to contribute?

Together, we can advance toward making purpose and people the heart of business.

November 2020   Hubert Joly

NOTES

Introduction

1. Lisa Earle McLeod, *Leading with Noble Purpose: How to Create a Tribe of True Believers* (Hoboken, NJ: Wiley, 2016).

Chapter One

1. Marcus Buckingham and Ashley Goodall, *Nine Lies about Work: A Freethinking Leader's Guide to the Real World* (Boston, MA: Harvard Business Review Press, 2019), Appendix A, 237–245.

2. Jim Harter, "Dismal Employee Engagement Is a Sign of Global Mismanagement," Gallup Workplace Blog, https://www.gallup.com/workplace/231668/dismal-employee-engagement-sign-global-mismanagement.aspx.

3. Gallup, *State of the Global Workplace* (Washington, DC: Gallup, 2017), 5.

4. Andrew Chamberlain, "6 Studies Show Satisfied Business Employees Drive Business Results," *Glassdoor*, December 6, 2017, https://www.glassdoor.com/research/satisfied-employees-drive-business-results/.

5. Glassdoor, "New Research Finds That Higher Employee Satisfaction Improves UK Company Financial Performance," March 29, 2018, https://www.glassdoor.com/about-us/new-research-finds-that-higher-employee-satisfaction-improves-uk-company-financial-performance/.

6. In a yearlong study conducted in 2016–2017, involving over 500,000 employees from 75 companies across 15 industries, Glint, a platform that measures and improves employee engagement, found that people who scored unfavorably on employee satisfaction were five times more likely to quit in the subsequent six months, and 12 times more likely to quit in the subsequent 12 months of the survey than those who scored neutral or favorably.

7. Buckingham and Goodall, *Nine Lies about Work*, Appendix A, 237.

8. Glint customer studies.

9. Aristotle's hierarchy of occupations ranked work—either servile or skilled—at the bottom, inferior to *praxis*, or putting ideas into practice, and to

theoria, or intellectual contemplation, considered the most noble way to spend one's life.

10. Roman poet Virgil tells the story of Jupiter making it necessary for humans to labor to satisfy their desires—unlike the gods, who were free from the burden of work. Cicero writes of work as vulgar, degrading body and mind.

11. "Cursed is the ground because of you; through painful toil you will eat of it all the days of your life," God tells Adam after he eats the apple from the forbidden tree (Genesis 3:17); and "By the sweat of your brow you will eat your food until you return to the ground" (Genesis 3:19). Looking at it this way, work appears to be necessary but painful.

12. Adam Smith, *Wealth of Nations* (New York, NY: Random House, 1937), 734–735.

13. In this view, work's only purpose is to earn a living, but work itself has no intrinsic utility. "Work is a necessary evil to be avoided," said Mark Twain. And according to Austrian journalist Alfred Polgar, "Work is what you do so that some time you won't have to do it anymore."

14. General Stanley McChrystal, Swith Tantum Collins, David Silverman, and Chris Fussell, *Team of Teams: New Rules of Engagement for a Complex World* (New York, NY: Portfolio/Penguin, 2015).

15. McChrystal, Collins, Silverman, and Fussell, *Team of Teams*.

16. According to the ADP Research Institute's global survey; see Buckingham and Goodall, *Nine Lies about Work*, 244–245.

Chapter Two

1. Khalil Gibran, "On Work," in *The Prophet* (New York, NY: Alfred A. Knopf, 1923).

2. Genesis 2:15.

3. This took the form of a number of papal encyclicals that ultimately got synthesized in the "Compendium of the Social Doctrine of the Catholic Church" published under John Paul II.

4. John Paul II, "Laborem Exercens," September 14, 1981, http://www.vatican.va /content/john-paul-ii/en/encyclicals/documents/hf_jp-ii_enc_14091981_laborem -exercens.html.

5. "All men were created to busy themselves with labor for the common good," said John Calvin.

6. John W. Budd, *The Thought of Work* (Ithaca, NY: Cornell University Press, Kindle Edition), 166. Also, Islam teaches that "the best of men are those who are useful to others" (162).

7. Budd, *The Thought of Work*, 166. Individuals are instructed to "strive constantly to serve the welfare of the world; by devotion to selfless work one attains the supreme goal in life" (162). And according to Gayatri Naraine, the Hindu spiritual educator and writer, "To add the dimension of service into work will put people at the heart of work, and fill it with a meaning and purpose that it often seems to lack." See Naraine Gayatri, "Dignity, Self-Realization and the Spirit of Service: Principles and Practice of Decent Work," in *Philosophical and Spiritual Perspectives on Decent*

Work, ed. Dominique Peccoud (Geneva, Switzerland: International Labour Organization, 2004), 96.

8. Andrew E. Clark and Andrew J. Oswald, "Unhappiness and Unemployment," *The Economic Journal* 104, no. 424 (May 1994): 648–659, https://www.jstor.org/stable /2234639?read-now=1&refreqid=excelsior%3Ab2ef5905f5bcbaad19ec08dd2dd565d7 &seq=11#page_scan_tab_contents.

9. Juliana Menasce Horowitz and Nikki Graf, "Most U.S. Teens See Anxiety and Depression as a Major Problem Among Their Peers," Pew Research Center, February 20, 2019, https://www.pewsocialtrends.org/2019/02/20/most-u-s-teens-see-anxiety -and-depression-as-a-major-problem-among-their-peers/.

10. Amy Adkins and Brandon Rigoni, "Paycheck or Purpose: What Drives Millennials?," Gallup Workplace, June 1, 2016, https://www.gallup.com/workplace /236453/paycheck-purpose-drives-millennials.aspx.

11. David Brooks, *The Second Mountain: The Quest for a Moral Life* (New York, NY: Random House, 2019).

12. Bill George, *Discover Your True North: Becoming an Authentic Leader* (Hoboken, NJ: John Wiley & Sons, 2015).

13. Hortense le Gentil, *Aligned: Connecting Your True Self with the Leader You're Meant to Be* (Vancouver, BC: Page Two, 2019). Hortense le Gentil is also my wife.

14. Gianpiero Petriglieri, "Finding the Job of Your Life," *Harvard Business Review*, December 12, 2012, https://hbr.org/2012/12/finding-the-job-of-your-life.

15. J. Stuart Bunderson and Jeffrey A. Thompson, "The Call of the Wild: Zookeepers, Callings and the Double-Edged Sword of Deeply Meaningful Work," *Administrative Science Quarterly* 54, no. 1 (March 2009): 32–57.

16. Dan Ariely, "What Makes Us Feel Good about Our Work?," filmed October 2012 at TEDxRiodelaplata, Uruguay, video, 20:14, https://www.ted.com/talks /dan_ariely_what_makes_us_feel_good_about_our_work.

Chapter Three

1. Marshall Goldsmith with Mark Reiter, *What Got You Here Won't Get You There: How Successful People Become Even More Successful* (New York, NY: Hachette Books, 2007).

2. Etienne Benson, "The Many Faces of Perfectionism," *Monitor on Psychology* 34, no. 10 (November 2003): 18, https://www.apa.org/monitor/nov03/manyfaces.

3. Brené Brown, *The Gifts of Imperfection: Let Go of Who You Think You're Supposed to Be and Embrace Who You Are* (Center City, MN: Hazelden Publishing, 2010), 7.

4. Brené Brown, "The Power of Vulnerability," filmed June 2010 at TEDxHouston, Texas, video, 20:04, https://www.ted.com/talks/brene_brown_the_power_of _vulnerability/transcript?language=en.

5. Jeff Bezos, "Annual Letter to Shareholders," April 6, 2016, US Securities and Exchange Commission, https://www.sec.gov/Archives/edgar/data/1018724 /000119312516530910/d168744dex991.htm.

6. Carol Dweck, *Mindset: The New Psychology of Success* (New York, NY: Random House, Kindle Edition, 2007), 20.

7. Thomas Curran and Andrew P. Hill, "Perfectionism Is Increasing over Time: A Meta-Analysis of Birth Cohort Differences from 1989 to 2016," *Psychological Bulletin* 145, no. 4 (2019): 410–429, https://www.apa.org/pubs/journals/releases/bul -bul0000138.pdf.

Chapter Four

1. A recent Edelman survey highlighted that a majority of respondents around the world believe that capitalism in its current form is now doing more harm than good, and according to the Pew Research Center, a third of Americans hold a negative view of capitalism. When asked why they think it is bad, they give two main reasons: the system is unfair and is responsible for wealth inequality; and, they argue, it is by nature corrupt and exploitative, hurting people and the environment. Although baby boomers still embrace free markets, young adults have grown noticeably more disenchanted with capitalism since 2010: only half now consider capitalism as positive—on par with socialism. See Edelman, "Edelman Trust Barometer 2020," 12, https://cdn2.hubspot.net/hubfs/440941 /Trust%20Barometer%202020/2020%20Edelman%20Trust%20Barometer%20 Global%20Report.pdf?utm_campaign=Global:%20Trust%20Barometer%20 2020&utm_source=Website; Pew Research Center, "Stark Partisan Divisions in Americans' Views of 'Socialism,' 'Capitalism,'" FactTank: News in the Numbers, June 25, 2019, https://www.pewresearch.org/fact-tank/2019/06/25/stark-partisan -divisions-in-americans-views-of-socialism-capitalism/; and Lydia Saad, "Socialism as Popular as Capitalism Among Young Adults in the U.S.," Gallup, November 25, 2019, https://news.gallup.com/poll/268766/socialism-popular-capitalism-among -young-adults.aspx.

2. In May 2016, *Time* magazine's cover article was about "American Capitalism's Great Crisis," which argued that "the U.S. system of market capitalism itself is broken." And in 2018, *The Economist* launched Open Future, an ongoing discussion about fixing the flaws of capitalism. See Rana Foroohar, "American Capitalism's Great Crisis," *Time*, May 12, 2016, https://time.com/4327419/american-capitalisms -great-crisis/; and https://www.economist.com/open-future.

3. Milton Friedman, "A Friedman Doctrine," *New York Times*, September 13, 1970, https://www.nytimes.com/1970/09/13/archives/a-friedman-doctrine-the-social -responsibility-of-business-is-to.html.

4. The Business Roundtable, "Statement on Corporate Governance," September 1997, 1, http://www.ralphgomory.com/wp-content/uploads/2018/05/Business -Roundtable-1997.pdf.

5. Edmund L. Andrews, "Are IPOs Good for Innovation?," Stanford Graduate School of Business, January 15, 2013, https://www.gsb.stanford.edu/insights/are-ipos -good-innovation.

6. Edelman, "Edelman Trust Barometer 2020."

7. BBC News, "Flight Shame Could Halve Growth in Air Traffic," October 2, 2019, https://www.bbc.com/news/business-49890057.

8. Larry Fink, "A Fundamental Reshaping of Finance," 2020 letter to CEOs, BlackRock, https://www.blackrock.com/corporate/investor-relations/larry-fink-ceo -letter.

9. Charlotte Edmond, "These Are the Top Risks Facing the World in 2020," World Economic Forum, January 15, 2020, https://www.weforum.org/agenda/2020 /01/top-global-risks-report-climate-change-cyberattacks-economic-political.

10. Lynn Stout, "'Maximizing Shareholder Value' Is an Unnecessary and Unworkable Corporate Objective," in *Re-Imagining Capitalism: Building a Responsible Long-Term Model*, ed. Barton Dominic, Dezso Horvath, and Matthias Kipping (Oxford, UK: Oxford University Press, 2016), chapter 12.

11. Global Sustainable Investment Alliance, "2018 Global Sustainable Investment Review," 8. What the Alliance considers "responsible investment" now accounts for a growing share of professionally managed assets in these regions, ranging from 18 percent in Japan to 63 percent in Australia and New Zealand (see p. 3). http://www.gsi-alliance.org/wp-content/uploads/2019/06/GSIR_Review2018F.pdf.

12. In June 2017, the Task Force on Climate-Related Financial Disclosures of the Financial Stability Board, an international body that monitors the global financial system, issued recommendations for banks, insurance companies, asset managers, and asset owners to disclose climate-related financial information in their public annual filings (see https://www.fsb-tcfd.org/publications/final-recommendations -report/). BlackRock has encouraged CEOs to adopt the recommendations. It has made it clear that it will vote against management and board directors of companies that are not making enough progress on such disclosures, as well as the business practices and plans that underpin them. See Fink, "A Fundamental Reshaping of Finance."

Chapter Five

1. Lisa Earle McLeod, *Leading with Noble Purpose: How to Create a Tribe of True Believers* (New York, NY: Wiley, 2016).

2. Simon Sinek, "How Great Leaders Inspire Action," filmed September 2009 at TEDxPugetSound, Washington State, September 2009, video, 17:49, https://www.ted .com/talks/simon_sinek_how_great_leaders_inspire_action.

3. Ralph Lauren, "About Us," https://www.ralphlauren.co.uk/en/global/about-us /7113.

4. Johnson & Johnson, "Our Credo," https://www.jnj.com/credo/.

5. Raj Sisodia, Jag Sheth, and David Wolfe, *Firms of Endearment: How World Class Companies Profit from Passion and Purpose*, 2nd ed. (Upper Saddle River, NJ: Wharton School, 2014), https://www.firmsofendearment.com.

6. Sisodia, Sheth, and Wolfe, *Firms of Endearment*.

7. See, for example, Cathy Carlisi, Jim Hemerling, Julie Kilmann, Dolly Meese, and Doug Shipman, "Purpose with the Power to Transform Your Organization," Boston Consulting Group, May 15, 2017, https://www.bcg.com/publications/2017 /transformation-behavior-culture-purpose-power-transform-organization.aspx.

8. Leslie P. Norton, "These Are the 100 Most Sustainable Companies in America—and They're Beating the Market," *Barron's*, February 7, 2020, https://www.agilent.com/about/newsroom/articles/barrons-100-most-sustainable-companies-2020.pdf.

9. Larry Fink, "A Sense of Purpose," Larry Fink's annual letter to CEOs, 2018, https://www.blackrock.com/corporate/investor-relations/2018-larry-fink-ceo-letter.

10. The companies whose CEOs are members of the Business Roundtable collectively employ more than 10 million people and generate over $7 trillion in annual revenues. https://www.businessroundtable.org/about-us.

11. Business Roundtable, "Statement on the Purpose of a Corporation," August 19, 2019, https://s3.amazonaws.com/brt.org/BRT-StatementonthePurposeofaCorporationOctober2020.pdf.

12. Business Roundtable, "Statement on the Purpose of a Corporation."

13. Global Justice Now, "69 of the 100 Richest Entities on the Planet Are Corporations, Not Governments, Figures Show," October 17, 2018, https://www.globaljustice.org.uk/news/2018/oct/17/69-richest-100-entities-planet-are-corporations-not-governments-figures-show.

14. "The American dream is alive, but fraying," says Jamie Dimon, chairman and CEO of JPMorgan Chase & Co. and chairman of Business Roundtable. "Major employers are investing in their workers and communities because they know it is the only way to be successful over the long term." Bill McNabb, the former CEO of Vanguard, echoes the same sentiment. "By taking a broader, more complete view of corporate purpose, boards can focus on creating long-term value, better serving everyone—investors, employees, communities, suppliers and customers." See Business Roundtable, "Business Roundtable Redefines the Purpose of a Corporation to Promote 'An Economy that Serves All Americans,'" August 19, 2019, https://www.businessroundtable.org/business-roundtable-redefines-the-purpose-of-a-corporation-to-promote-an-economy-that-serves-all-americans.

Chapter Six

1. Kavita Kumar, "Amazon's Bezos Calls Best Buy's Turnaround 'Remarkable' as Unveils New TV Partnership," *Star Tribune*, April 19, 2018, http://www.startribune.com/best-buy-and-amazon-partner-up-in-exclusive-deal-to-sell-new-tvs/480059943/.

2. Kumar, "Amazon's Bezos."

3. V. Kasturi Rangan, Lisa Chase, and Sohel Karim, "The Truth about CSR," *Harvard Business Review*, January–February 2015, https://hbr.org/2015/01/the-truth-about-csr.

4. Marc Bain, "There's Reason to Be Skeptical of Fashion's New Landmark Environmental Pact," *Quartz*, August 24, 2019, https://qz.com/quartzy/1693996/g7-summit-new-fashion-coalition-unveils-sustainability-pact/.

5. Marc Benioff and Monica Langley, *Trailblazer: The Power of Business as the Greatest Platform for Change* (New York, NY: Random House, Kindle Edition, 2019), chapter 2, 26–33.

6. Jim Hemerling, Brad White, Jon Swan, Cara Castellana Kreisman, and J. B. Reid, "For Corporate Purpose to Matter, You've Got to Measure It," Boston Consult-

ing Group, August 16, 2018, https://www.bcg.com/en-us/publications/2018/corporate
-purpose-to-matter-measure-it.aspx.

Chapter Seven

1. Statista, "Small Appliances," n.d., https://www.statista.com/outlook/16020000
/109/small-appliances/united-states.
2. We did not yet know that the presentation would eventually be pushed back to
November 13 because of Hurricane Sandy.

Chapter Eight

1. Richard Schulze, *Becoming the Best: A Journey of Passion, Purpose, and Persever-
ance* (New York, NY: Idea Platform, 2011), 153.
2. RSA Animate, "Drive: The Surprising Truth about What Motivates Us,"
YouTube, filmed April 1, 2010, video, 10:47, https://www.youtube.com/watch?v
=u6XAPnuFjJc&feature=share.
3. Daniel Pink, "The Puzzle of Motivation," *TEDGlobal 2009*, video, 18:36,
https://www.ted.com/talks/dan_pink_the_puzzle_of_motivation/transcript?referrer
=playlist-why_we_do_the_things_we_do#t-262287.
4. As far back as the early 1970s, research by Edward Deci, a professor and
chairman of the Psychology Department at the University of Rochester, concluded
that payment for performance undermines what is known as "intrinsic
motivation."
5. Samuel Bowles, "When Economic Incentives Backfire," Harvard Business
Review, March 2009, https://hbr.org/2009/03/when-economic-incentives-backfire.

Chapter Nine

1. Shawn Achor, Andrew Reece, Gabriella Roser Kellerman, and Alexi Robi-
chaud, "9 out of 10 People Are Willing to Earn Less Money to Do More-Meaningful
Work," Harvard Business Review, November 6, 2018, https://hbr.org/2018/11/9-out
-of-10-people-are-willing-to-earn-less-money-to-do-more-meaningful-work.
2. Bill George, *Discover Your True North: Becoming an Authentic Leader* (Hoboken,
NJ: John Wiley & Sons, 2015).

Chapter Ten

1. Dan Buettner, "How to Live to Be 100+," filmed September 2009 at *TEDxTC*,
Minneapolis, MN, video, 19:03, https://www.ted.com/talks/dan_buettner_how_to
_live_to_be_100.
2. Charles O'Reilly and Jeffrey Pfeffer, *Hidden Value: How Great Companies
Achieve Extraordinary Results with Ordinary People* (Boston, MA: Harvard Business
School Press, 2000).

3. Raj Sisodia, Jag Sheth, and David Wolfe, *Firms of Endearment: How World Class Companies Profit from Passion and Purpose*, 2nd ed. (London, UK: Pearson Education, 2014), 68.

4. John Mackey and Raj Sisodia, *Conscious Capitalism: Liberating the Heroic Spirit of Business* (Boston, MA: Harvard Business Review Press, Kindle Edition, 2012), chapter 15.

5. This is what Amy Edmonson, professor at Harvard Business School, identified as "psychological safety."

6. Drake Baer, "Why Doing Awesome Work Means Making Yourself Vulnerable," FastCompany, September 17, 2012, https://www.fastcompany.com/3001319/why -doing-awesome-work-means-making-yourself-vulnerable.

7. Brené Brown, "The Power of Vulnerability," filmed June 2010 at *TEDxHouston*, TX, video, 12:04, https://www.ted.com/talks/brene_brown_the_power_of_vulnera bility?language=en.

8. Mackey and Sisodia, *Conscious Capitalism*, 227.

9. Dorie Clark, "What's the Line between Authenticity and TMI?," *Forbes*, August 26, 2013, https://www.forbes.com/sites/dorieclark/2013/08/26/whats-the-line -between-authenticity-and-tmi/#12881ca720a9.

10. Marriott International, "A Message from Arne," Twitter, March 20, 2020.

11. McKinsey & Company, "Women Matter, Time to Accelerate: Ten Years of Insights into Gender Diversity," October 2017, 13–15, https://www.mckinsey.com/~ /media/McKinsey/Featured%20Insights/Women%20matter/Women%20Matter%20 Ten%20years%20of%20insights%20on%20the%20importance%20of%20gender%20 diversity/Women-Matter-Time-to-accelerate-Ten-years-of-insights-into-gender -diversity.ashx; and Vivian Hunt, Dennis Layton, and Sara Prince, "Why Diversity Matters," McKinsey & Company, January 2015, https://www.mckinsey.com/business -functions/organization/our-insights/why-diversity-matters.

12. McKinsey & Company, "Women Matter."

13. Jen Wieczner, "Meet the Women Who Saved Best Buy," *Fortune*, October 25, 2015, https://fortune.com/2015/10/25/best-buy-turnaround/.

14. Sally Helgesen and Marshall Goldsmith, *How Women Rise: Break the 12 Habits Holding You Back from Your Next Raise, Promotion, or Job* (New York, NY: Hachette Books, 2018).

15. Stephanie J. Creary, Mary-Hunter McDonnell, Sakshi Ghai, and Jared Scruggs, "When and Why Diversity Improves Your Board's Performance," Harvard Business Review, March 27, 2019, https://hbr.org/2019/03/when-and-why-diversity -improves-your-boards-performance.

16. Clare Garvie and Jonathan Frankle, "Facial-Recognition Software Might Have a Racial Bias Problem," *The Atlantic*, April 7, 2016, https://www.theatlantic.com /technology/archive/2016/04/the-underlying-bias-of-facial-recognition-systems /476991/.

Chapter Eleven

1. Robert Rosenzweig, "Robert S. McNamara and the Evolution of Modern Management," Harvard Business Review, December 2010, https://hbr.org/2010/12/robert-s-mcnamara-and-the-evolution-of-modern-management.

2. Daniel Pink, "Drive: The Surprise Truth about What Motivates Us," RSA Animate, April 1, 2010, https://www.youtube.com/watch?v=u6XAPnuFjJc.

3. Robert Karasek, "Job Demands, Job Decision Latitude, and Mental Strain: Implications for Job Redesign," *Administrative Science Quarterly* 24, no. 2 (June 1979): 285–308, https://www.jstor.org/stable/2392498?casa_token =zErCV0xkAv8AAAAA:YpBVSvBEQ5hj7z_EYgfGGX4QUUVJO4LhV_vTcm2lTXPj OuYoQqlzLkzmzvwfd4jL5SlhKnbv6ZejaHhIY_vDHolTkpjZjiN2hQ4Dj9VRXlcYur _6ab9bCA&seq=1#metadata.

4. Amazon, Jeff Bezos's letter to shareholders, April 2017, https://www.sec.gov /Archives/edgar/data/1018724/000119312517120198/d373368dex991.htm.

5. Paul Hersey and Ken Blanchard developed this model of "situational leadership." See Paul Hersey, Kenneth Blanchard, and Dewey Johnson, *Management of Organizational Behavior: Leading Human Resources*, 10th ed. (Upper Saddle River, NJ: Pearson Prentice Hall, 2012).

6. Alex Berenson, "Watch Your Back, Harry Potter: A Wizardly Computer Game, Diablo II, Is a Hot Seller," *New York Times*, August 3, 2000, https://www.nytimes.com /2000/08/03/business/watch-your-back-harry-potter-a-wizardly-comuter-game-diablo -ii-is-a-hot-seller.html.

Chapter Twelve

1. George Leonard, *Mastery: The Keys to Success and Long-Term Fulfillment* (New York, NY: Penguin Publishing Group, Kindle Edition, 1992), xiii.

2. Neil Hayes, *When the Game Stands Tall, Special Movie Edition: The Story of the De La Salle Spartans and Football's Longest Winning Streak* (Berkeley, CA: North Atlantic Books, 2014).

3. "Our right is limited to the performance of the action entrusted to us, and our duty lies in performing it to the best of our ability. When our mind is focused on the fruit of the action, instead of the action itself, we tend to be distracted and unable to give our full attention. Obsession can also make us nervous, and the need to win drains us of power." From Menon Devdas, *Spirituality at Work: The Inspiring Message of the Bhagavad Gita* (Mumbai, India: Yogi Impressions Books, Kindle Edition, 2016), 103.

4. Robert Sutton and Ben Wigert, "More Harm than Good: The Truth about Performance Reviews," *Gallup*, May 6, 2019, https://www.gallup.com/workplace /249332/harm-good-truth-performance-reviews.aspx.

5. Rosamund Stone Zander and Ben Zander, *The Art of Possibility: Transforming Professional and Personal Life* (New York, NY: Penguin), chapter 3.

6. Marcus Buckingham and Ashley Goodall, *Nine Lies about Work: A Freethinking Leader's Guide to the Real World* (Boston, MA: Harvard Business Review Press, Kindle Edition, 2019), 111.

Chapter Thirteen

1. Chan Kim and Renée Mauborgne, *Blue Ocean Strategy: How to Create Uncontested Market Space and Make the Competition Irrelevant* (Boston, MA: Harvard Business School Publishing, 2004).

2. This phrase was developed by authors James Collins and Jerry Porras.

Chapter Fourteen

1. Emma Seppälä, "What Bosses Gain by Being Vulnerable," Harvard Business Review, December 11, 2014, https://hbr.org/2014/12/what-bosses-gain-by-being-vulnerable.

2. Rodolphe Durand and Chang-Wa Huyhn, "Approches du Leadership, Livret de Synthèse," HEC Paris, Society and Organizations Institute, n.d.

3. Clayton Christensen, "How Will You Measure Your Life?," Harvard Business Review, July–August 2010, https://hbr.org/2010/07/how-will-you-measure-your-life.

4. Christensen, "How Will You Measure Your Life?

Chapter Fifteen

1. Clayton Christensen, "How Will You Measure Your Life?," Harvard Business Review, July–August 2010, https://hbr.org/2010/07/how-will-you-measure-your-life.

2. Marshall Goldsmith and Scott Osman, *Leadership in a Time of Crisis: The Way Forward in a Changed World* (New York, NY: Rosetta Books, 2020).

Conclusion

1. Hortense le Gentil, *Aligned: Connecting Your True Self with the Leader You're Meant to Be* (Vancouver, BC: Page Two, 2019), 2.

INDEX

ACKNOWLEDGMENTS

Hubert Joly

I owe a huge debt of gratitude to quite a few individuals who have played a major role in making this book a reality.

I am incredibly grateful to:

- The many sources of inspiration I have had over several decades. Several of my McKinsey clients, such as Jean-Marie Descarpentries and Yves Lesage, have taught me fundamental principles of leadership. Father Samuel has been a constant spiritual guide and source of inspiration and wisdom to me for over three decades now. Marilyn Carlson Nelson showed me how it is possible to lead with love. Russ Fradin, a partner of mine at McKinsey who was later the lead independent director at Best Buy, has generously shared his wisdom with me over the years. Marshall Goldsmith has had a huge impact on my life in general and on my ability to open up to feedback and get better in particular. Eric Pliner later helped me learn more about effective team leadership. Jim Citrin of Spencer Stuart not only helped me get the CEO job at Best Buy but has also been a regular source of intelligence and wisdom about leadership and growth. Ralph Lauren has been a role model for me, showing me how you can build a business around the dream of a better life. Bill

George has been a mentor, a thought partner, and a role model for more than 10 years now; he has also shared invaluable feedback at various stages of the development of this book, and penned its foreword. More broadly, many great CEOs as well as business and nonprofit leaders I have gotten to know over the years have been wonderful sources of inspiration for me about how to lead from a place of purpose and humanity. A good number of them have generously provided kind words of endorsement for this book too.

- The entire Best Buy team. I have learned so much from my friends and colleagues at Best Buy, starting with the company's founder, Dick Schulze, and long-time CEO Brad Anderson, whom I first got to know as a board member at Carlson; all the Best Buy executives and leaders mentioned in the book, especially my wonderful successor Corie Barry, who may be one of the foremost CEOs in the world today; every member of the Blue Shirt Nation I have had the chance to work with and learn from (you have given me so much!); and last but not least, each director of the company, especially my friend Hatim Tyabji, who was non-executive chairman when I joined.

- The team at HEC Paris with whom I have partnered around the Joly Family endowed Chair in Purposeful Leadership. Thank you, Peter Todd and Professor Durand, for believing in these ideas and using them to help reshape business education.

- My new colleagues at Harvard Business School for welcoming me as a professor and giving me the opportunity to help prepare the next generation to become great leaders and tackle the challenges the world is facing.

- Caroline Lambert, my writing partner, who has been a delight to work with and made it all happen. If writing a book is not hard, writing a good book is extremely difficult. To the extent this one is good, much of the credit goes to Caroline.

- Rafe Sagalyn, my agent, who kept pushing us to sharpen the "arc of the book," encouraged us persistently to "show, not tell," and ultimately introduced us to the wonderful team at HBR Press.

- The team at HBR Press, especially Scott Berinato, our amazing editor, with whom Caroline and I had the pleasure of collaborating throughout the project. His guidance and support along the way have been invaluable. Scott, we loved every one of our working sessions with you.

- My wonderful assistants Shelley Plunkett, Marcia Sandberg, and Ysadora Clarin, who have supported me with grace and effectiveness before, during, and after this project.

And I am especially grateful to my parents, who have taught me the importance of hard work and decency, to my children for their love, their ideas, and their encouragement, and to Hortense for her miraculous support and partnership.

Caroline Lambert

Working on this book has been a joy and an inspiration.

Thank you, Hubert Joly, for inviting me to share your book adventure. And what an adventure it was! We made it through several relocations, major life changes, a global pandemic, Wi-Fi breakdowns, and countless hours over Zoom. Thank you for trusting me with your ideas and stories, for responding to my questions and prodding with such grace, and for offering an inspiring vision of business—so very different from the corporate world I fled many years ago. Thank you also for your patience, kindness, generosity, and positivity. I could not have dreamed of a better book partner.

We were incredibly lucky to have Scott Berinato, our editor extraordinaire, with us from the very beginning. These pages greatly benefited from his feedback and sharp editing, and his humor and encouragement made our meetings a joy. Thank you to the entire HBR Press team too, for helping move this book from computer screens to bookshelves.

Several peer reviewers were kind enough to read the manuscript and give valuable feedback. Thank you!

Rafe Sagalyn, Hubert's agent, generously helped us refine the proposal and found our publishing home at HBR Press.

My heartfelt thanks to Shelley Plunkett, Marcia Sandberg, and Ysadora Clarin, who organized the logistics of our meetings month after month. Thank you to Matt Furman and his team for helping us with Best Buy material.

I owe a sizable debt of gratitude to Hortense le Gentil, without whom none of this would have happened. Thank you, Hortense, for your continued friendship and support.

Finally, my deepest gratitude and love go to my husband, David, and our daughter, Zoe, for their love, support, and understanding throughout late nights, drafts, and revisions. My world starts and ends with you.

ABOUT THE AUTHORS

HUBERT JOLY is best known as the former chairman and CEO of Best Buy. During his time there, he and his team rebuilt the company into one of the nation's favorite employers, a sustainability leader, and an innovator, vastly increasing customer satisfaction and dramatically growing the company's stock price. His greatest achievement, however, may have been to make himself dispensable: he decided to step down as CEO in 2019 and as executive chairman in 2020, and pass the baton to a new generation of leaders.

Hubert Joly joined Best Buy in 2012 armed with no experience in retail but having successfully led a number of company transformations, both in his native France and in the United States. He has been recognized as one of the one hundred "Best-Performing CEOs in the World" by *Harvard Business Review*, one of the top thirty CEOs in the world by *Barron's*, and one of the top ten CEOs in the United States in Glassdoor's annual Employees' Choice Awards.

Hubert's purpose in life is to make a positive difference on people around him and use the platform he has to make a positive difference in the world. Besides serving on the boards of Johnson & Johnson and Ralph Lauren, he now spends most of his time as a senior lecturer at Harvard Business School and supporting other leaders seeking to become the best versions of themselves and to lead with purpose and humanity. He is also actively invested in efforts to advance meaningful diversity and inclusion.

Writing collaborator **CAROLINE LAMBERT** has helped a wide range of change makers and thought leaders in business, civil society, and politics translate their ideas and experience into books. Previously a foreign correspondent and deputy Asia editor at *The Economist*, she wrote about business, economics, and politics in various parts of the world, earning the Diageo Africa Business Reporting Award and the Sanlam Award for Excellence in Financial Journalism. Caroline holds an MBA from INSEAD and an MA in international relations from the Johns Hopkins University's School of Advanced International Studies, where she received the C. Groove Haines Award in International Policy. She is a former Visiting Fellow at the Center for Global Development.